THE MYS

A CONVERSA

TAYLOR LEWANDOWSKI

Published in the United States by:
Archway Editions
a division of powerHouse Cultural Entertainment, Inc.
32 Adams Street, Brooklyn, NY 11201

www.archwayeditions.us

Daniel Power, CEO
Chris Molnar, Founder and Editorial Director
Nicodemus Nicoludis, Founder and Managing Editor
Naomi Falk, Senior Editor
Mia Risher, Publicist

Copyedited and Proofread by Liz Janoff and Tyler Considine,
Arts Editing Services

Library of Congress Control Number: 2024949891

ISBN: 9781648230936

Printed by Toppan Leefung

First edition, 2025

10 9 8 7 6 5 4 3 2 1

Printed and bound in China

ARCHWAY
EDITIONS

THE MYSTERY OF PERCEPTION

A CONVERSATION WITH LYNNE TILLMAN

TAYLOR LEWANDOWSKI

Archway Editions, Brooklyn, NY

Advance Praise

"Lynne Tillman and Taylor Lewandowski thrillingly retrace a life in letters spanning vast terrain, from novels to film; from Warhol's Factory to Japan. A master class in retrospection and an invaluable lens on Tillman's oeuvre, for fans and scholars alike."

KRITHIKA VARAGUR

"This conversation stars Lynne Tillman's uncanny memory of people, places, and events with subjects and topics ranging from Jane Bowles, Sigmund Freud to Madame Realism, Tillman's witty fictional cultural commentator. *The Mystery of Perception* amplifies her unparalleled voice and perspective on literature, art, and culture. Lewandowski is an astute interlocutor. I loved every word."

LAURIE SIMMONS

"A wise woman (Lynne Tillman) said, 'No one wants to see you air your clean laundry in public,' but here she is, and what she exposes is a novelist's curiosity: Why is one person different from another? She moves—in conversation and in her fictions—with deep musicality, impeccable phrasing and timing. How do our perceptions refract through the phantasmagoria? How does reading a book or making a friend shape our inner life? Lynne Tillman is an intrepid explorer of consciousness—the perilous terrain of other and self."

ROBERT GLÜCK

"The mind of Lynne Tillman is a trove of insight, which she graciously displays in her work, but also, lucky for us, in this fantastic conversation."

NATASHA STAGG

"If being a writer is a superpower, because of her care and teaching and mentorship, she is a huge part of my origin story, the radioactive spider, the gamma ray, that unlocked something new. Lynne Tillman is one of the great thinkers and creatives of our time. She is one of a kind, and it is a delight to have these conversations that illuminate her genius."

NANA KWAME ADJEI-BRENYAH

"Writers on writers. Taylor Lewandowski, who has read all of Lynne Tillman's books ('Oh, you have?' she says), interviews the New York mainstay at length. Tight and quippy, edited brilliantly, this book is full of gossip, notes on craft, and everything else that makes up a writer's life."

FIONA ALISON DUNCAN

"This interview situates the vast imagination and invention of Lynne Tillman's literary contributions alongside a (chosen) family album of fellow artists and writers, correcting the record from that time period that heretofore only cites the men. To read the interview feels like sitting across the kitchen table from an old friend. One loses themself in her stories to find they have arrived at moments of true knowledge accrued from lived experience and an acrobatic mind."

JUSTINE KURLAND

CONTENTS

"Though skeptical and prone to depression, I write in the hope and spirit that each of us can think beyond our limits, while acknowledging our limits. I picture us all . . . with many possible voices. There are identities, there are shifting subjectivities, and you and I are shifty subjects who may from time to time be many things, not essentially one thing, except by desire perhaps and in certain moments, for certain reasons and for certain periods of time. I really am looking for new narratives to replace the old ones. I distrust words and stories and yet probably they are what I value most. Paradox rules."

Lynne Tillman, "Critical Fiction/Critical Self," 1991

The Funniest Person I Know

Andrew Durbin

Lynne Tillman's *No Lease on Life* (1998) follows twenty-four hours in a woman's fight with her New York City landlord, the narrative interrupted occasionally—clocked, as it were—by jokes. A favorite of mine: "It's a small world, someone said to Jackie Curtis. Not if you have to clean it, Jackie Curtis answered."[1] Here, between the harangues and harassments, humor keeps the score of a wry Manhattan at the end of the century, when the passage of plague expunged Lynne's East Village of some of its greatest talents and invited in the real estate speculators. "We only laugh when a joke has come to our help," Sigmund Freud writes in *Jokes and Their Relation to the Unconscious* (1905), a line Lynne quotes in the middle of the novel.[2] Jokes keep alive the feeling of a place and its dialect, which has long concerned her as a novelist and essayist of "these intemperate times," as she once put it.[3] What was life like, how did it sound?

For Lynne, writing is almost always a social act, just like telling a good joke. To make someone laugh is to ask them to come closer, to do exactly what every great novelist does: She invites you in. Lynne tells Taylor Lewandowski in this book-length conversation that she once asked friends what she should write about next. Cynthia Carr encouraged her to "come home" to New York after she had set two books in Europe, so she decided to take Carr's advice literally and set *No Lease on Life* on her block in the East Village. But where's home for Lynne, who speaks here about how important her years abroad were to her formation as a thinker, how far afield her mind remains? To call her a "downtown writer" (a term she dislikes) has always misapplied geography to an artist without much patience for the confines of neat categories; her apartment might be downtown, but she lives in the world. She tells Taylor, "I think of myself as an oppositional writer." That means living—and writing—on the edge, from up in the eaves and under the floorboards: a difficult place from which to work. But then I suspect it is necessary for the vantage it gives her on modern life, whatever that may be. Only from the outside can you see the absurdity.

"I've always been very curious about people other than myself," Lynne tells Taylor. "I wanted to know how things happen, why people think the way they do, and why certain events happen, and the antecedents. I'm always frustrated, because, of course, I can't absorb everything."

Some read Lynne for her narrative experimentation; some for her combining criticism and fiction; some for her brilliant portraits of men and women fascinated—and troubled—by images, the images they make of themselves, the images they make of others. Of course, I read Lynne for all that, but I also read her for a good laugh, because the author of *American Genius, A Comedy* (2006) and *Someday This Will Be Funny* (2011) is very, very funny. Of all the praise rightly accorded to her fiction and nonfiction over the years, her humor tends to earn the least mention among critics, which has always puzzled me. Though none of her novels or short stories are written in a satiric or comic mood, they are often hilarious, even if the hilarity is typically Tillmanesque—rather oblique.

A good joke depends on good timing. Lynne's sense of timing (she is always probing what it means to be on—and in—time) is complicated, innovative. Consider how the narrator of her novella *Weird Fucks* describes the end of one of many flings in the early 1970s: "By now everyone knows that Valium is one way to get over a love affair. After taking those pills long enough, life becomes intensely fair: everything is the same."[4] Except it isn't, of course. A few chapters later, we return to regular programming when, with more sex, the importance of unfairness (always a determining condition for whether something is funny) reasserts itself: "I should have known better," she tells us. "Upper middle class guys from Westchester are trouble and can't fuck."[5] These sly and subtle jokes—you don't have to laugh out loud to know they're funny—play out as nervous comedy, a comedy of tics: Are you really supposed to smile at this American girl trudging compulsively from guy to guy? Yet in offering a smirk at the dismal and the absurd and even the pathetic in our lives, Lynne resembles another great literary humorist, Franz Kafka. He, too, doesn't get enough credit for how funny he is.

Kafka flirted and fell in love through humor. He courted Felice Bauer by reporting farcical stories about his colleagues at the Workers' Accident Insurance Institute, and he spent weeks wooing Julie Wohryzek by telling jokes at a sanatorium.[6] At work, he was known for his uncontrollable laughter. Once, the mere sight of a chief executive at the Institute prompted a concerning fit of giggles.[7] His fiction is also a riot. Remember the hotel elevators in *Amerika*? Or, in "A Report to an Academy," the ape's homily on freedom, how he praises with such seriousness the goodness of his captors for not beating him for his carrying fleas aboard their ship? When Kafka read aloud from the first chapter of *The Trial* to a group of friends, he was so overcome with laughter he couldn't finish it. His friends were astonished because the text struck them as so very grave. "But that is how it was," Max Brod wrote, with the flat astonishment of a medieval chronicler.[8] Kafka, too, laughed when a joke rushed to his side, for the cruelties of modern life—there was the soulless alienation of office work and the horrors of the First World War—is not without its need for black humor. Even in the ghettos and camps of the 1930s and '40s jokes were popular; it is often laughter, not prayer, that delivers us from evil.[9]

When I first met Lynne, we spent a summer evening at an Italian restaurant in the West Village giggling over something probably no one else would have found funny. In a performative mood, I reenacted a bad night with a mutual friend, an old drunk—known in the literary world for his self-denial and boozing—who had fallen over at a hotel from too many goblets of wine, leaving me to drag his limp body to a cab while an entire hotel lobby looked on piteously. This ended the friendship. Someday this will be funny, I told myself. It was Lynne who showed me it was. Learning to joke about yourself is one of the ways you become a writer: Humor is how she teaches writing, she tells Taylor.

Laughter provided our friendship with its early purpose. In our first lunches and dinners and phone calls that followed, we were always testing out ways of making the other laugh, either with a joke or, better yet, the occasional indulgence in good gossip or some salty observation of our surroundings. We have laughed at things that we know will take our friends a while to catch up to: We laugh at discomfort, absurdity, struggle. We have laughed because we are in each other's company, and the shared memory of some woman's ridiculous laugh outside a Second Avenue trattoria, a curious phrase another writer once wrongly used catches us again. I wish I could bottle Lynne's laughter, for it is more than a sound that has carried me this past decade, it is an atmosphere in which life becomes easier to breathe because it is lighter, clearer, more bearable. This is the source of the Kafkaesque in Lynne's fiction, her humor: It is laughter that shatters the sea frozen within us.

Lynne once wrote that laughing is a "form of love."[10] It is what saves her from sad thoughts, and it salvages relationships. "Maybe it's also my form of self-medicating," she says, "because I need it most when I'm feeling down."[11] Her humor makes me feel less alone. I think of one moment—it is quintessentially Tillmanesque—in my favorite of her novels, *Motion Sickness* (1991). In that book, she observes that the Pepsi ad, "Come alive—you're in the Pepsi generation", was translated in Thailand to mean "Pepsi brings your ancestors back from the dead."[12] Recalling this linguistic flub leads her narrator to wonder whether she is alive and to quip that if a mere sip of soda can resurrect dead relatives, then no one must be haunted anymore. Problem solved: A can of Pepsi, please! Of course, no amount of Pepsi can bring back the dearly departed, so its promise is false, though no less funny and no less provocative. But then humor is a release from suffering, she says, and from what haunts us, our obscure past, our unreadable future. It's like what Kafka's ape says in his report: Laughter and play give access to our shared humanity, a feeling so powerful it can knock buildings down. That's when Lynne Tillman, with dark hilarity, comes to rescue us from the ruination.

Why Lynne Tillman?

Taylor Lewandowski

In Lynne Tillman's debut novel, there's an eponymous epigraph from the poet H.D., from *Tribute to Freud*: "We are all haunted houses." This idea is in every person. Our separate worlds. Our many rooms. Our sentimental memories. Our traumatic incidents. Doors locked and unlocked. Tidy closets. Cluttered closets. Unfinished basements with objects buried so deep we may never unearth them. A complicated question hovers over Lynne's five-decade-long career: How do I understand "I"? This question creates a vacuum-like energy. This is evident in Lynne's far-reaching preoccupations with art, photography, sociology, psychoanalysis, American history, family, and, of course, literature itself. The "I" Lynne uses to form narratives predicated on consciousness unravels the fact our thoughts are not our thoughts; they are images constantly in flux. This concentration on individuals in a destabilized world overwhelmed with stimulation creates an important portrait of our modern American life. It creates a multitude of selves, possibilities within us all, however violent, misleading. Reality will only increasingly become more obscure, more populated with images; it will only mutate as time progresses. It's rare to be confronted by work so concerned with these complications. Lynne uses her precursors, like Franz Kafka, Jean Rhys, Jane Bowles, Virginia Woolf, Harry Mathews—to name a few—and forms a necessary amalgamation informed by artists and friends, like Susan Hiller to form narratives for our present age and for those to come—far surpassing most contemporary American writing.

I first heard of Lynne Tillman in my early twenties. I listened to episodes of her conversations with Michael Silverblatt on *Bookworm* as a custodian in Chicago. I remember attending the Brooklyn Book Festival in 2014. I watched Ben Lerner read from *10:04* and Sam Lipsyte from *The Fun Parts*; A. M. Holmes on a panel; and Tom Wolfe walking through the book fair, his infamous white suit against the usual participants' tote bags and *Paris Review* merch. I recall crossing a street and walking past Lynne Tillman. It's funny to memorialize a moment so disconnected from me in this moment—as if these memories happened to a different Taylor during a different era. It wasn't until I was living in Montana that I found her collection of essays *What Would Lynne Tillman Do?* (2014) in a used bookstore that I earnestly began to read her. It was a quick introduction: Paula Fox, William Eggleston, Andy Warhol, Peter Dreher, Edith Wharton.

Fast forward to 2022, and I'm reading with Lynne at KGB Bar with Stephanie LaCava and Gideon Jacobs, hosted by Em Brill. I didn't anticipate this, but I felt an immediate rapport with her, which I'd later come to find as an essential Lynne trait: an impassioned curiosity. After the reading, all of us had dinner at The Odeon. I sat between Gideon and Lynne, and we talked about literature, New York City, Edmund Wilson (which surprised me then but now does not), and other cursory topics. *The Mystery of Perception: A Conversation with Lynne Tillman* was born out of this evening at The Odeon.

The question still isn't answered. Why Lynne Tillman? Even Lynne asked me this several times, "Why me?" Tillman has published six novels, five short story collections, two essay collections, two books on New York City culture, codirected and wrote a film about Frances Farmer, and more books yet to come. I think Lynne's proximity to writers like Harry Mathews and Paul Bowles early on in her career provided not a stylistic influence, but early examples that guided her own writerly aspirations. It's this similar proximity I followed at first with a blind obsession, which has evolved into a touching familial affection for Lynne, admiration for her work and spirit (and I admit a model for me personally), and a deep recognition of a person deeply invested in the world around her. As I read her work, I found a mind in constant dialogue—one that is not concerned with easy answers. In most of her fiction, she circles around the idea of perception. She uses various masks and carves out idiosyncratic voices. In her essay "Ugly," she describes the value of fiction as inventing "other possible realities . . . other ways to think, other outcomes, futures, pasts, to fantasize what's vile or beautiful or in-between, to let loose unconscious desires, to dig at boundaries, to foray into uncontrollable, to poke at what's repressed, to try to unearth it—the unwanted, the awful, the ugly." Tillman has always centered this approach. Her characters struggle to unravel their illusions. They humorously stride through life in a world that does not make sense.

In *Haunted Houses* (1987), there are three voices, three girls struggling to wrestle with their present lives, but more importantly society's expectations. In our conversation, Lynne describes wearing large men's khaki pants so often in college that she wore them out in the inner thigh and, not knowing how to sew, pinned pieces of T-shirts to the pants. This, along with other instances in her early life, illustrate a person always rebelling against usual assumptions. She unpacks the complication of gender and arrives at a natural fluidity. This is explored in Lynne's decision to write from a gay man's consciousness in *Cast in Doubt* (1992) and Ezekiel Hooper Stark, the "New Man" born under the sign of feminism, in *Men and Apparitions* (2018) but also the multiplicity of women in different eras, ages, and cultural backgrounds. She says in the conversation: "I wasn't going to become a conventional 'woman.' I wasn't going to be a man or woman, neither was what I wanted to be. I didn't like the attributes. I didn't want to be masculine or feminine. I wanted to make my own decisions, even if I didn't know they were decisions." This early disconnection from her sense of self and her surroundings created a force that did not immediately transpire into works of fiction. As Tillman describes in the conversation, it wasn't till her exposure to visual artists and writers like

David Rattray, Gary Indiana, and Susan Hiller, along with years in psychoanalysis, that enabled her to transmute her ideas into writing, even though this impulse existed early on in grade school.

In her short story collection, *This is Not It* (2002), which pairs Lynne's short stories with contemporary art, "The Undiagnosed" is another example of her creating doubt in the assumed fixed binary of gender. Coupled with a photograph by Linder Sterling of two people wearing shoes, one of which is dirty working boots and the other clean leather boots with spurs on a hardwood floor, the story begins with the narrator attending a costume party in a ballroom. She wears her father's clothes. Lynne writes, "No one at the party knew what man I was, and, like so much of life, it was only in my head. Costumed, I felt I could not be myself, which had obscure benefits." The narrator moves through the ballroom as if in a dream. She begins to reflect on her father, even though she doesn't want to: "I wiggled uncontrollably in my father's suit. I didn't want to think of his body." She later thinks (in a characteristic Lynne Tillman sentence):

> I remembered the long, dark hairs on his forearms, the hairlessness of his upper arms and chest, his hazel, illegible eyes, his uneven, uncontrollable mouth, his penis when he urinated, and dressed as a man, I began thinking about men I'd known, and wondered casually, noticing other costumed miscreants and misfits, if I could remember every one of them who mattered to me, and even those who hadn't and didn't at the time when time was unimportant, and if I could see them in my mind's eye and reckon with their foreign, familiar bodies, their alien, similar lives. I'd been raised as a woman. I didn't feel I was one, and I didn't care that I didn't.

The narrator acknowledges the ancient feeling of not belonging in one's self. The story shifts when Clint Eastwood enters the ballroom. How could it not? "I wasn't surprised to see him, I'd been expecting him for years. Sometimes I conjured him after watching one of his movies and then in dreams I knew him intimately." The narrator nervously watches Clint Eastwood interact with other men in the ballroom. She observes everyone in the room is dressed as someone they want to be or someone they don't want to be. Eventually, Clint and the narrator talk to one another. He tells her about his father digging a deep hole and living in it as a kind of protest—to prove his manhood. They discuss Eastwood's *Unforgiven* and the narrator's own need to slay her father, "as in days of yore." In "The Undiagnosed," Lynne utilizes the introspection of the narrator, Clint Eastwood, and the ballroom circumstance to demonstrate the father's chokehold on the psyche, the fluctuating register of gender, and a blurry definition of an "I."

In *American Genius, A Comedy* (2006) and *Men and Apparitions*, Lynne's style and concerns sharpen into dense representations of consciousness against illusions. They are similar to "The Undiagnosed" and her past novels, but they are far greater in their scope. Tillman intricately designs these novels to contain the character's thoughts, ideas, images, cultural signifiers. They muse on Leslie Van Houten, textiles, dermatology, skin care, Eames chairs, Frederick Jackson Turner, the Zulu alphabet, Franz Kafka, Clifford Geertz, Virginia Woolf, family photographs, Clover Hooper Adams, and much more. Both of these novels are a culmination of her consistent project to render consciousness on the page. In *Men and Apparitions*, Tillman finds the perfect structure and bite-sized pacing that engenders a special propulsion in contrast to her other novels. It also incorporates her thinking on photography, her friends and colleagues, i.e. Laurie Simmons, Cindy Sherman, and Stephen Prina. Through the perspective of an ethnographer of family photographs, Ezekiel Hooper Stark, Lynne reflects on the unfixed position of an image among his own struggles with love and belonging. She has evolved the representation of the "I" into a complex, pleasurable novel. Once the family is explored and deconstructed by Zeke, Lynne uses this as a vehicle to delve deeper into the complications of our childhood surroundings and biological inheritance. The individual swimming in an overstimulated disarray of signs, relations, dialogue. How do I relate to you?

It's this mystery of perception Lynne and I discuss sporadically: Our pasts buried in the biology. The makeup of who we are in any given moment—the haunted house of the self. The possibility of de-education, as Lynne describes it via Franz Kafka, knowing your thoughts are not your thoughts. Lynne's focus on the multiplicity of "I" is not an autobiographical concern but an investigation into what it means to be American, or simply human. It's a great gift to step into the world of Lynne Tillman, and I hope this accompanying conversation is a companion to her work.

Except for the first sessions in her East Village apartment, most of these interviews were conducted via phone from April 2023 to January 2024.

the PARANOIDS' BALL

MUDD CLUB March 22 77 White St. 10:30 pm

MASKED BALL

Publication Party/Benefit for

Paranoids Anonymous Newsletter

With: Bob Carroll, Lindsay Smith, Martha Wilson, Heinz Emigholz, Rene Ricard

Admission **$5** includes copy of P.A.N. #3

Dress optional, masks obligatory

I. Who Are You?

Mr. Gorchov ○ The Vocation ○ Performance as Contention ○ The Background is Always Present ○ No Literary Expectations ○ New York Chitchat

Lynne Tillman: We're talking about *Paranoids Anonymous Newsletter*. I was so shy and terrified to show my writing, so publishing "Diary of a Masochist" anonymously was perfect. That was my first long story, apart from "Living with Contradictions" published in 1982 by Top Stories—Jane Dickson illustrated it.

Taylor Lewandowski: *Didn't David Rattray work on the* Paranoids Anonymous Newsletter *as well?*

He put in an anonymous story. Actually, when the first *Paranoids* came out, Leonard Lopate invited us on his midnight radio program. We went on wearing masks, even though it was radio. Lopate thought it was very funny. David Rattray said at some point, "The devil exists." It was a hilarious night. I'm sure there's no record of it. [*coughs*] This isn't a cold. It's seasonal allergies.

It's the beginning of allergies for me.

Do you want a Claritin?

No, I'm fine. It's not overwhelming.

It's never hit me before. But when I went up to Hudson last week to teach, as soon as I got off the train, my throat and nose felt scratchy. I was told by allergy sufferers that this is a very heavy pollen season, because there was little snow last winter.

How did you meet David Rattray?

He came into my life fifty years ago. 1970. I was living in Europe. Maybe it was '71. I was living in Europe, where I stayed until 1976 (this is after college). I only came back to the States twice. I really thought I was an expatriate.

You lived there from '70 to '76?

'69 to '76. Almost seven years. I came back and it just so happened that night I went to St. Mark's Poetry Project, and Patti Smith went electric for the first time, you know, with Lenny K. I'm not a great fan of hers, although I like her singing, because I think her attitude toward women—it's probably changed, she does have a grown daughter—but it was all men she'd mention as writers. There was never a woman in there. Now there's Emily Dickinson. The safe choice for all misogynistic women. [*laughs*] Or Sylvia Plath. They're the go-to women. Both of whom I love. So, David was sitting right behind me at this Poetry Project thing. He was alone. I was alone. I liked going to things alone. I always have and I always will. He was sitting behind me. Somehow we got to talking. He tapped me on the shoulder. We went over to Max's, but he'd been eighty-sixed. He wasn't allowed in. He was an alcoholic. He wasn't on dope yet, I think.

He later got sober, right?

at the Whitney and

from René Ricard

we just at Peto + Cabrage

Dear Lynnie— I just
got me a brand new
camera + this was the
picture the sales Aren't
woman made:
I dramatic: Love xxxxxx

Lynne Tillman
29 JOHN ST.
NY 10038

USA 10¢
Iolani Palace
Honolulu
Hawaii
Historic Preservation

Well, he'd go on and off the wagon. He worked at *Reader's Digest*. The interesting thing about it was he kept this job, and I don't know if he kept this job then, but he was an editor for encyclopedias or dictionaries or something like that. All of us had his number at *Reader's Digest*. You'd call him up with questions like, "What's the Polynesian saying for . . . ?" He knew everything. He was always teaching himself a new language to the very end. But he was fun. He could be outrageous. I think at first he had a crush on me. I think he fell in love with a lot of women and men. There was a long period when he was mad for this one guy. I forget his name, but he was also married with a kid. But he kept that job, and it sustained him and his family for years and years. He was pretty amazing. He once said to me drinking was much rougher on the body than heroin. I think he was probably right. Like Alex Trocchi. I knew Alex Trocchi. He was in pretty good shape. That's when I was living in London. One day I'll write that story.

About him?

About him. Yeah. Anyway, I left for Europe after college. I knew I'd never be a writer if I stayed home.

Mr. Gorchov

Where did you go to college?

Hunter. Right here in the city.

What did you study?

English literature and American history. I took all my electives in studio art, which had an enormous impact. You could do that. Hunter had a great art department, so I worked with Ron Gorchov, who died not long ago in his nineties. I was madly in love with him, of course. I fell in love with all my male art teachers. I don't think I had any women art teachers. There weren't any then. And Doug Ohlson. He was a minimalist. Ron, I always called him Mr. Gorchov, but toward the end of his life I was finally able to call him Ron. It was ridiculous, everyone else called him Ron.

My oldest sister and her second husband helped me get to Europe. He was in the travel business. I traveled around for six months, and stayed in a London hotel until they kicked me out, because I brought a guy back. The staff all hated me. I had no idea how obnoxious it was to be the sister-in-law of a guy who did business with the hotel. I was blissfully unaware. I got up late, so I kept the breakfast room open longer than they wanted. One of my regrets, behaving like that. So, they kicked me out. I really did not want to go back to America.

You went to London, then Amsterdam?

I traveled all around. Actually, I landed first in Amsterdam.

This is when you stayed in Crete and acted in Charles Henri Ford's Johnny Minotaur?

Yes, that period. Did you watch the whole thing?

Most of it.

Isn't it awful?

You can only watch it on this porn site.

MoMA restored it. I don't think they knew what was in it, but it was Charles Henri Ford and he was fascinating. I had ended up at Charles's house with a guy I was traveling with, and Charles asked me to be in his film. Of course, I said yes.

Wait. How did you meet Charles?

I was at the Spanish Steps and a Greek named Stephanos came up to me and said, "You must go to Crete! You are beautiful, and Charles Henri Ford will want to put you in his film!" I didn't know what I was doing, so I went to Crete, and Charles Henri Ford put me in his film. Anything was an opportunity, a reason to go one place or the other. I didn't know what the hell I was doing. I knew, of course, I had to be a writer.

The Vocation

When did you want to be a writer?

When I was eight. It feels like a fable now, but it's true. It happened. In third grade, our teacher assigned us an essay to write about Charlemagne. I was in a cushy, suburban place in Long Island. We had very good teachers. I don't regret that I didn't go to private schools, because it was an excellent school. Forty of us received New York State scholarships. We had good teachers. I wasn't a good student until my junior year.

I started writing "Charlemagne, Man of Peace." I was very excited writing it. I wrote another essay titled, "Charlemagne, Man of War." So, you see my ambivalence and contrariness appears very early. [*laughs*] I knew then I was a writer. I knew I could be a good writer. I just knew it. An infamous story, and a fact. I went to my mother and said, "I'm going to be a writer." She said, "But I didn't think you had

any talent." And that was my mother. Little did I know how jealous she was. I was eight years old. I didn't believe her, Taylor. That's the thing. She was already mean and nasty to me. I was fortunate. If she was one of those slap-kiss mothers, inconsistently loving me, then hating me, I'd probably be psychotic, but she didn't do that. I knew she was wrong. I knew I was talented. Whatever talent is. I knew I had it. That was it. Isn't that strange? I was going to be a writer.

When I was ten, my sisters (who are six and nine years older) and I all received Royal portable typewriters. A friend of a friend's father was an executive at Royal Typewriters, so my father bought three of them. Mine was fire engine red. I should've kept it. It was beautiful with chunky, white keys. From then on, I never wrote by hand. Only typed. But I never learned to type, which was stupid. Basically, I believe an identity formed around the fact that I'd become a writer. I could do this. Through all the misery and doubt, what kept me going was the feeling I had to do it. One of my analysts said, "You had a calling." Well, if you want to call it that, that's fine, but I never thought of it like that. I'd like to think it's true.

The impulse was always there.

Yes.

At a very young age, I remember reading The Three Musketeers *in my first-grade classroom. I wasn't reading it for content, but reading it for style. I liked how the words looked on the page. I wasn't comprehending all of it, but I was into the idea of experiencing text. That's how literature has always worked for me in some ways. This tangible, imaginative space. It eventually, of course, morphed into something else. It was my own private world.*

It was a place where I could be by myself, away from my family, which was a very fractious, difficult family. When I was ten, I felt confined,

closed in by the suburbs. I recognized I was depressed. I remember thinking about clothes and the fact I had to wear a different outfit every day in high school. So, when I got to college I bought a pair of large men's khaki pants and wore them exclusively until they were worn through at the inner thighs. I didn't know how to sew, so I cut up pieces of a T-shirt, pinned it up there, and they'd flap open. [*laughs*] This was my rebellion against having to look a certain way every day. I found it so horrible. That's why I hated shopping. I never wanted to shop, but the girls and probably boys in my high school seemed to shop all the time. Everything changed when a friend of mine, Lois, a person I loved, was killed in a car crash at the beginning of my junior year. I confined myself, I was in mourning and didn't know it, and I started to take high school seriously. In literature, books, I wasn't confined. I was in a different world. This was freeing. Oddly enough, and I know that summer camp for many was a horrible time, but for me I was given a taste of what it would be like not to live in Woodmere. To have different friends. Not to be with my family. And for two months in the summer I'd go away and feel like a different person. Early on, I recognized I had to change where I was in order to make other changes. Very important to me. I never wanted to go home. I'd weep like mad. It was not a happy home. Not at all. Then high school. Oh my god.

I can easily imagine suburbia, or family for that matter, as a form of confinement. I grew up in a Christian, conservative environment. Literature acted as a buffer. I could exist on family vacaions and be completely cut off from the world around me.

Marvin Taylor, who started the Downtown Collection at the Fales Library, came from a tiny, tiny town. He found everything, books, opera. His world became art and music. His knowledge of literature is exceptional. Where are you in the pecking order?

Performance as Contention

I'm the oldest.

Not surprised. I'm the youngest, but there were years between us, and, frankly, I don't think I would've survived without those gaps. Anyway, David Rattray. He was important to me for several reasons. We read each other's work. He'd come over and read to David Hofstra and me. He was translating Crevel's first novel, *Difficult Death*, which is wonderful. We would roar with laughter. In the beginning, it's so funny. He'd read it in a very arch tone. I wish I would've recorded it.

David Rattray was also one of the first readers of *Weird Fucks*, when I started working on it in '76. David and I stayed in touch. Back in New York, I saw him again. So from let's say '76 on, we were close. He loved *Weird Fucks*. I tried to get *Difficult Death* published, and this is interesting. It's the late eighties by now. He could not get it published. And by '86 or '87, I asked Edmund White to see if his press would publish it. At the end of *Difficult Death*, the protagonist, a gay man, commits suicide. So, no, it was not a positive image. They would not publish it.

No one would publish Difficult Death, *especially at that time.*

Yes, at that time with AIDS and the demand for positive imagery, which is a shitty problem. I think every minority group goes through this and probably has to. How to represent? That's why Dennis Cooper had such problems. I recently wrote an introduction to the new edition of his first novel, *Closer*.

Really?

For Serpent's Tail in London. Dennis said it revealed ideas in *Closer* he hadn't thought about, which is what happens when someone else reads your work seriously and closely. The first time I read it, I found it comical, a comedy. The second time I read it I experienced it very differently. Not a tragedy, but something else entirely. It was an interpretation, he said, that hadn't been made.

His work is really funny. People don't often see the humor in it.

It is funny in a mordant way. I went to an interesting panel at the CUNY Graduate Center. On one panel were young gay writers, of whom Dennis was the oldest, and on the other panel were older gay writers, including Richard Howard, Ed White, Allen Ginsberg, and a couple of others, all of whom were published and most well known. At the end, there was a Q&A. I was one of maybe ten women, otherwise all men. And someone in the audience asked Dennis a question about sex in his novels. Dennis said, "I am terrified of sex." You could hear an audible gasp. In the era of sexual freedom, no one said they were terrified. Everybody was supposed to be "liberated." And if you didn't get the way he writes about sexuality, as in *Closer*, which is a part of what I wrote about, you don't see there is little to no pleasure. His mention of terror—that was revelatory for people who were misreading his work, or missing that. One doesn't want to be a determinist. You must read it this way, but at least you have to see, from the horror and violence in his novels, that sex is not easy, free, or fun. His boys don't have beautiful sex. We're friends and supporters of each other, which might seem strange given that our writing is so different, but he likes a lot of different kinds of writers, and so do I. He's a wonderful, very generous man, and very gentle. People don't expect that.

The other reading was Frisk, *and he had . . .*

It was at the Kitchen on West 19th Street. Dennis went first, then Mary Gaitskill. Dennis had five other men read his piece from *Frisk*, like a play. After Dennis finished, Kathy whispered, "That was horrible. What's happened to Dennis?" Dennis walks over to say hello to us, and Kathy turns her back to him. Dennis was really hurt. It was inexplicable, except that she was recently back in New York, maybe felt alienated, out of place. Probably it came from great insecurity. You can be celebrated, the way Kathy was, but insecurity never leaves you. Then Mary read from *Two Girls, Fat and Thin*. Mary had told me before it was published, our first books were published by Poseidon, it was influenced by *Haunted Houses*. She never explained how, except there were two girls in it, and *Haunted Houses* had three. But that can't be it. [laughs] The Ayn Rand material in it, I found politically odd. I'd read Rand's novel, *The Fountainhead*, years ago, and thought it was kind of proto-fascist. The desire for strong men. "Who is John Gault?" I hadn't thought about Rand in years. I saw Rand as an American Leni Riefenstahl, but that may be extreme.

I haven't read that novel.

I don't think many do. Mary is a compelling contrarian. I liked *Bad Behavior* and *Veronica* a lot. So, Mary gets up to read. I believe she was on crutches; she had a broken leg. When she reads, her ass rotates. It's kind of like she's doing the twist. It's funny. We laughed about it later. Both readings pissed off Kathy, and, after that night, she wouldn't speak to me. It was very upsetting, but later we reconciled. Kathy, for all that she had and was, with many readers who adored her work and still do—she was insecure, competitive, and troubled. Not that unusual for an artist. (Laughs) I think toward the end of her life in San Francisco, she found her people and became much happier. I was in touch with her after this unhinged break. On a panel at a conference with her in Buffalo—what was it about? The new Gothic. Interest in it had emerged because of Patrick McGrath's fascinating *The Grotesque*, Patrick is a wonderful writer and old friend. On the panel, Kathy was distant, but it was a start. There were other times we saw each other, and it was friendlier. When she was dying in Mexico, I called her. It was a loving call. Very sad.

You mention Kathy Acker's insecurity. Did you have your own early insecurities?

Yes, from very early in my life, and especially in college, for many reasons, including and most importantly, an unhelpful childhood. I wasn't totally insecure, because I knew I had to write when I was eight. That's not insecure. It's odd, insecurity. Almost every artist I know is insecure. For one thing, you're making something that you want to think is "good," but you don't know. Standards shift, the chosen in one moment are unchosen in another. Some get prizes, some don't. Some get lauded in print, others ignored or smashed. People go on. Writers write, and feel, at least I do, that nothing is alive without writing. Jane Bowles, think of her. Her doubts paralyzed her. Paul Bowles said she couldn't cite a cantilevered bridge if she didn't know everything about its mechanics. There was great praise for *Two Serious Ladies*, for me it changed the field, but her massive doubts didn't stop. And they often don't. Look at Kafka, except he made his doubts and angst function. Still, Jane Bowles died miserably, after five years in a Spanish hospital following a debilitating stroke. I received some encouragement, especially from my eighth-grade teacher, Mrs. Bloch. It was a terrible year for me, awful. I was very depressed, friends ganging up on me, and Mrs. Bloch asked the class to write the ending of a famous story that had allowed for two endings, two possible doors. I wrote my heart out and came up with a third door. I don't remember it. My parents threw out almost everything when they sold the house in Woodmere. Mrs. Bloch asked me to read the story to the class. I was startled, and did it with terror and anarchic pride, because I knew my so-called friends would hate my recognition from Mrs. Bloch. So, you're interested, mostly, in my friendships?

The Background Is Always Present

Well, no. I mean, sort of. There's an essay in David Rattray's How I Became One of the Invisible, *"On Spirals," which uses the spiral as a way to drive towards a deeper understanding, so I am thinking about how this concept, or image of the spiral connects to your psychoanalytic novels, like* American Genius, A Comedy *and* Men and Apparitions. *In your interview with Michael Silverblatt on* Bookworm, *you talk about psychoanalysis and how these novels are not psychological, but psychoanalytical. Do you believe in the subconscious?*

Unconscious. Subconscious doesn't exist. Freud got rid of that concept. Yes. I do believe we have material in our minds of which we are unaware, upon which we act without acknowledgment. I think that's why being in psychoanalysis or psychoanalytic psychotherapy has been so important. The old bugaboo: It's going to take away my demons. No, it's going to let 'em loose. Artists sometimes say, "My creativity is within my demons." That's sad stuff to me.

That's why I like Rattray's essay, where he's talking about falling deeper into the spiral. Those two novels are all about consciousness and using these various things like skin care, photography, family to move below the surface and hopefully closer to a core understanding. These characters are constantly intellectualizing, often to their own detriment. They can't fully exorcize their demons or alleviate their anxiety.

With *Men and Apparitions* specifically, I wanted to connect unconscious desire and behaviors with conscious choices, feelings with theories. Like, why is he interested in family photographs? It's not simple, but first it's because of his relation to his father, to his mother, to his family without ever saying that. It's not that I want to talk about someone's psychology. I'm interested in the reality we choose if we

think we're choosing something freely. It's not that it's completely involuntary or voluntary. It's that the unconscious, the environment, the background is always present.

Do you think the closer we move toward the unconscious, it leads us to who we're supposed to be?

Who we're supposed to be? Getting closer to the unconscious, no, but sometimes an unconscious motivation is revealed. What psychoanalysis asks for is understanding. It's not a cure. It's being able to talk to yourself: Why did I get so angry at so-and-so? What is it that's upsetting me? Being able to analyze or understand, to some extent, your own behavior keeps you, one, from being a victim and, two, able to proceed differently, hopefully. One of the things that's so awful about American life, politics, or discourse is how reactive it is. Everybody has to react. You can't say, "Actually I don't know enough," or, "I don't know what I think."

Everybody thinks they have to be one of those talking heads, everybody repeats what the heads say. It's not once you know you have an unconscious . . . It's just trying to understand why something has hurt you, for instance, how you are complicit, why you get into situations you do, choose friends that you do—now I avoid narcissists as much as possible, so I stay home more [*laughs*]—or why you react in a certain way that, seeing it, might allow you to make a change, maybe. Understanding yourself. It's not a simple thing. It's never complete. I'm angry at so-and-so, but the why could lead to another reaction, so that your behavior will not already be determined.

Do you lean more towards Freud or Jung?

Freud. I'm not a Jungian at all. I once saw the funniest Jungian movie, where every time anyone was talking about the unconscious, they went into an elevator that went down to the basement. [*laughs*] No, I don't believe in anima and animus. Female and male properties.

Did you ever read Alice Notley's The Descent of Alette?

No, no.

It's inspired by the Tompkins Square Park riot that happened.

Yeah, in '89. I was here. I should read it.

You were in your apartment?

Suddenly, I heard helicopters. I thought I was in Vietnam. It was horrible.

Wow. I was thinking about that book while walking through the park to get here. The deeper she goes into this underworld, or subway system of New York City, the closer she becomes to a true self who must battle this male figure, this Tyrant. At the end, she arrives at the surface, the Tyrant is vanquished, and everyone arises out of the bulwark of the city, like a new birth.

There's no true self.

I don't know if I agree.

What is a true self?

I feel like there's this potential Taylor. There is the image, like you mention, the images we create, and I feel there are decisions I make that move towards that person, or maybe it's just another image.

I don't think I move toward myself, that there is a self waiting, or that it is more or less honest or true. I think every day, more likely, I repeat myself, otherwise I'd confuse myself and friends. [*laughs*] Every day I think we make it up. That's my form of existentialism. Don't you feel like you're different with different people? Have you ever been in any psychoanalysis?

I see a therapist every week.

What kind of therapist?

She's more aligned with Jung.

I was trying to write consciousness in both novels and maybe in all my work. Like Horace in *Cast in Doubt*. Have you ever read that?

Yes, definitely. I've read all of your books.

Oh, you have?

The last one I just finished was Bookstore: The Life and Times of Jeannette Watson and Books & Co. *We have to talk about that.*

I never really wanted to write that book.

I can imagine, but it's a beautiful book.

People really like it.

It's important.

No Literary Expectations

It's a cultural history of a particular time in the New York literary world. I think the reason why I'm an odd writer is because I'm inconsistent. I remember a critic complaining. She had read *Cast in Doubt* and said, "Now you write *No Lease on Life*, and it's so different. How can I talk about your work?" Furious with me. Well, they're different concerns, but there's a belief that a writer has one style. You can say Rothko is working, painting, in a certain vein. Whatever you write and go more deeply into that, I'm all for it. I always wanted to change it up and give myself another problem.

Your capacity and concerns are so wide. Not every writer is like that. I saw a photo of you and William Kennedy on Instagram. I haven't read a lot of his books, but I think of him as a . . .

A solid, traditional novelist. Yes, he is. He's a wonderful man. He's a modest man. He was friends with Norman Mailer and all of these people.

To be honest, I didn't even know he was still alive.

He's ninety-three or ninety-four now. I saw him not long ago. He's very present. He's now dealing with his wife's Alzheimer's. Horrible.

Yeah. My grandma's experiencing that right now.

Memory loss, brain damage. Have you read *Mothercare?*

Oh, yes.

Bill never got a big head. He was awarded a MacArthur and started the Writer's Institute at the University at Albany. He's a really good man.

He's a straight-ahead, solid writer. He knows his territory. The people in Albany revere him, so do I.

That's so different from you, because you move through so many worlds. You absorb all this material.

I've always been very curious about people other than myself. I think from an early age I was seeking people outside my family. I wanted to know how things happen, why people think the way they do, and why certain events happen, and the antecedents. I'm always frustrated, because, of course, I can't absorb everything. I surround myself with books, some of which I've read, some half read, and some not. It's like the way I buy certain products for my skin. I buy them, but I don't use them, but knowing I have them is a great comfort. [*laughs*]

Definitely. That's how I feel about books.

Yesterday I read a part of a book on Velázquez for something I'm writing right now. If it turns into anything, some of the novel will be about him and "Las Meninas," which will be the second time I'll be writing about that work. I'm interested in many different things. I wish I had more time.

I think this impulse to want to absorb everything works in tandem with your curiosity. Dialogue, interviews have always been important in your work.

New York Chitchat

Conversation is very important. Living in New York City, as much as everyone disses the place, I still find I can have conversations with special and interesting people. People are expected, in a way, to converse. Once at a dinner, after an opening, four of us were sitting at a table, one of whom was a former curator at MoMA, and no one was saying anything. Boring. I say, "Look, we're in New York City. We're meant to talk to each other. Let's have a conversation." I actually did that. [*laughs*] And so we did. I disagreed almost violently with the curator, who was a big deal. His attitude drove me crazy. At least, we were not just making chitchat, which also drives me crazy. I'd rather learn something about somebody else. I'd rather hear your whole history than talk about nothing. Or myself.

II. You Know Yourself In Relation to Others

American Writer ○ **The Stranger** ○ **Prior Models (Harry Mathews)** ○ **Your Thoughts are Not Your Thoughts** ○ **Technology and Gender** ○ **Becoming** ○ **Indiana Detour** ○ **Jane Bowles** ○ **Contextual Differences** ○ **Reading as Analysis**

Lynne Tillman: It was John Waters's birthday yesterday.

Taylor Lewandowski: *That's right.*

He reads everything. He read my work way before I would have imagined. You know his quote, "If you go home with a guy and there are no books, don't fuck him"? Love it. I was speaking to a friend of mine at lunch. He's gay, or queer, but I think he'd call himself gay. He's in his sixties and single, but doesn't want to have sex, even though he's on PrEP, without using condoms. He says in Europe that's fine. People accept it, even want to use condoms. Here, the younger guys don't want to use them. All these STDs spreading again. Mpox. It's compelling, the risks people take for pleasure. He doesn't want to get syphilis. You look worried.

American Writer

Oh, just thinking. So, returning to William Kennedy. What do you think it means to be a New York writer? Do you consider yourself one?

I guess I am, but I don't think of myself as a New York writer. Actually, I'm an American writer. I say this because many years ago the first translation of *Haunted Houses*—actually the only one—was in German. Hannes Hatje was translating it, and was not a regular translator, but a very complex artist. He'd ask me questions, like, "What is a push-up bra?" and other things that made me realize they were American phrases, words. *Oh*, I thought, *I am an American writer.*

Of course, I'm called a "New York City writer," but the only New York novel I have written was *No Lease on Life*. That was deliberate. I chose to write a New York City book. Dennis Cooper thinks this is very funny, that I sometimes asked people, not trying to be like Warhol: "What do you think I should write about? What would interest you?" Again, writing is a social act. It's obvious. It's private and personal, but it's also social. I bumped into Cynthia Carr, who wrote the great David Wojnarowicz biography, and now has a book on Candy Darling. I said, "I just don't know what to write next. I'm stymied." This was after *Cast in Doubt* was published. She said, "Why don't you come home? Your last two books were set in Europe. We need you here." Well, I thought, wow. I had written a short story in the late eighties for the Carnegie International in Pittsburgh titled "Other Movies." It's in my first collection. There was so much work of appropriation in that show, I thought I'd do an appropriation, so I appropriated all the characters on my block. [*laughs*] And turned them into movie characters.

This block?

Oh, yes—this block. I thought about that earlier story, which was about my neighborhood, and thought no one on this block would have read it. Woe is me, one of them had, but he was quite nice about it. I had made him a mafia boss. [*laughs*] So *No Lease on Life* was born from that. That's my New York City novel, but *American Genius: A Comedy*, *Cast in Doubt* . . . I mean, isn't there a distinction between the crowd you hang with, or the group you're with . . . those of us who've been linked together I think have some affinities in writing, Gary Indiana, myself, or Eileen Myles, anti-establishment, anti-middle-class pieties. In the 1980s, critic Robert Siegle wrote *Suburban Ambush: Downtown Writing and the Fiction of Insurgency*, the first work on this group. He was prescient, I think.

Of course that's not just true to New York, those groupings and affinities. But that term is a brief way for reviewers, booksellers to brand a book. Like autofiction, dirty realism, all of these descriptors. I'm in a losing war against them.

I think of myself as an American writer, because I think about America. I think about America's problems, democracy for one, and issues that drive all my books. In my first full-length novel *Haunted Houses*, three American girls of different classes represent different American values, and have overarching, at least in the West, experiences. The girls become socialized as women. Of course they're all rebellious. I think of myself as an oppositional writer. I remember someone saying my writing wasn't like Richard Hell's. It didn't look rough. Instead there was a patina or a kind of elegance to the writing, or it wasn't sloppy. It wasn't part of the ethos then: You don't know how to play guitar, start a band.

I watched Downtown '81 *last week. Did you ever see this?*

Who made it?

Glenn O'Brien.

Oh, I probably did.

Basquiat walks around the city, but I mention it because some of the bands are terrible.

The Stranger

David Hofstra played with a number of bands, including The Contortions with James Chance. Although, his heart was not in punk but R&B and jazz. He's a great bass player.

How did you two meet?

In a bar—the old way. Tribeca before it was really Tribeca. We met . . .

What year was that?

'77. We've been together . . . It's shocking. You never expect anything like that. Most of my life I've lived with this man. Who is he? One time I came home and he was in a bad mood and I said, "Why can't I come home and you talk to me as if I'm a stranger? Say hello, or just be nice even though you're in a bad mood." I went into our front room and sat on the couch. He goes to the kitchen and comes to the front room, and says, "I think I have to call the police." I said, "Why?" He said, "Because there's a stranger on the couch." [*laughs*] That's the glue. He was interviewed in the first issue of *Bass Player* magazine in 1990. We'd been together years, and when the issue came out, this was its premier issue, and there he was in a feature article. The writer had asked him, "How do you know what to play?" because bass players often make up their part. He said, "When I don't know what to play, I find something to leave out." That's like me. I realized that aesthetically we were linked. It was fascinating to find that out. I couldn't live with a writer, not because we're a miserable lot, but because I don't want to talk about writing all day.

You never dated a writer?

Americans Abroad, an anthology of writings from American
expatriates, was edited by Peter Neagoe and published in
The Hague by Servire Press, 1932. Included in it are
pieces by Caresse and Harry Crosby, Gertrude Stein, Djuna
Barnes, Ezra Pound, Cahrles Henri Ford (see his book of
7 Poems in this exhibit) and many others. Servire Press
also published some issues of transition, edited by Eugene
Jolas.

I liked this book so much, I decided to make another "expatriate" anthology. I was then living in Amsterdam.
The book was to have been published in Holland in 1974
but the company to publish it disbanded. It is now being
published by Cold Turkey Press, Rotterdam, due out the
end of 1978. Included in the anthology is an unpublished
page from her notebook by Jane Bowles, letters to his
mother (1931) by Paul Bowles, a diary piece from Charles
Henri Ford, and many other never-before published stories,
poems, essays from Harry Mathews, Bill Levy, Marvin Cohen,
Carla Liss and others.

The second Americans Abroad can be subscribed to in advance and as the edition will be limited, if you are
interested in subscribing, please contact Lynne Tillman,
29 John Street, Room 1606, NYC 10038 for details.

Did I seriously date a writer? No. Not seriously. A couple wanted to—I had a date with a poet, he bored me, I probably bored him. Harry Mathews said to me in front of his wife, "Why didn't you ever sleep with me?" [*laughs*] I said, "Harry . . . "

It seems like you and Harry were close.

We were.

You have some books dedicated to him.

He was very important to me. He was also a complicated friend in some ways.

Prior Models (Harry Mathews)

How was he important to you?

He was really the first published writer who befriended me. When I was living in Europe and Amsterdam in the early '70s, I had been given a gift for my birthday, a book called *Americans Abroad*. It was published in The Hague in 1932. In English. Stein was in it and Harry and Caresse Crosby. Most of these writers are no longer talked about, they're unknown. I wanted to edit a collection of *Americans Abroad* for the present. I had a Dutch publisher. Peter B. was a character and lusted for six-hundred-pound women. A little guy, he wanted to be smothered, he told me. I fear suffocation. Anyway, he liked the idea and gave me fifteen hundred guldens. Back then, that was a nice amount. I was making no money and living hand-to-mouth. Never had my own place. Eventually, his "novelty" imprint failed, so my book was in limbo. I had never been an editor before. I was young. I read about Pound and Eliot. I thought you were supposed to tell people what you thought. Wow, did some people get angry. I wrote them rejection letters, explaining why. I learned very quickly just to reject. Of course, now I look at it and think how pompous. But you read these histories and think that's what an editor does. You let a writer know why you don't want the piece.

I didn't know anyone in Paris, so I wrote Maxine Groffsky, who was an editor at *The Paris Review*, and asked for names of American writers in Paris. She sent me three names. Sarah Plimpton, who was George's sister, which I didn't know. She wrote poetry. Harry Mathews and David Plante. Later, Plante wrote a book called *Difficult Women: A Memoir of Three* and one was Jean Rhys, whom he knew toward the end of her life. He was moralistic and really nasty about her. The hatred of women is, I don't know, it seems endless. And infuriating. Not enough people think about domestic violence, how many women are murdered every year, and raped in this country. Few really get it, this, I want to say, constant "pogrom."

Rhys is one of the greatest twentieth-century modernist writers. Brilliant. Still doesn't have her due. She's not on everyone's course reading list. Her last book was *Wide Sargasso Sea*, which did receive a lot of attention, and the one before that, *Good Morning, Midnight* is superb. Her use of language is amazing. Her writing is very important to me. But, anyway, collecting writers for the ill-fated anthology was how I came to know Harry Mathews. We corresponded. That's also how I met Paul Bowles. Thank goodness, it never was published, because it became horrible. I kept adding people. I couldn't say no. But there is an unpublished fragment by Jane Bowles I'd like to publish one day. Maybe give it to *n+1* and write about it. I hope I can find it.

Oh, yeah. You have to.

Paul found it in her archive in Texas and sent it to me for the anthology.

How did these writers, like Paul Bowles and Harry Mathews, influence you? I know Paul Bowles had an impact, especially because of Jane Bowles and the saga of trying to adapt Two Serious Ladies.[1]

First, Paul's writing didn't influence me. I liked his books, and in person he could be hilarious. I think Harry's experimentation with narrative influenced me. Not the way he wrote, but that he continued to write narratives against the flow of anti-narrative. Oh, the film, that nightmare. A movie has not yet been made. I'm glad I was stopped, because I turned a short story into *Motion Sickness*. I used a grant from the New York State Council of the Arts from from the film division. I gathered together $40–50,000 of grants to make *Two Serious Ladies*. I'm probably the only person to have sent money back to the Jerome Foundation.

You sent the money back?

They had given me $20,000, and I knew I wasn't going to make the film. I had spent about $2,500 going to Morocco to meet Paul. But "idiot" is the word for sending it back. They never even thanked me. [*laughs*] And for the NYSCA, B. Ruby Rich was running the film part of NYSCA. I wanted to send $20,000 back, but she said, "Lynne, it'll just go back to the State. Give me a proposal for something else." So, I proposed writing *Motion Sickness*, and with that I quit my proofreading job.

Your Thoughts Are Not Your Thoughts

And Motion Sickness *is really about your time traveling in Europe.*

Yes—it is very much fictionalized. I blended different times. It was a pleasure to write. I didn't have to do any research for *Motion Sickness* or

FEB 10 1986

Lynne Tillman
P.O. Box 360
New York, New York 10009

This will confirm information disclosed at your visit
January 29, 1986.

Our search in the appropriate Copyright Office
indexes and catalogs that include works cataloged
from 1938 through 1971 under the title THE COLLECTED
WORKS OF JANE BOWLES and the name Jane [Auer] Bowles
disclosed the following separate registration for a
work identified under this name and specific title:

COLLECTED WORKS, by Jane Bowles. With an introduction
by Truman Capote. Application states "Plain
Pleasures", pp. 297-431, previously published abroad
1966 and registered AI 10112. Registered in the name
of Jane Bowles, under A 968540 following publication
November 30, 1966.

Facts of registration for the other work in your
request are as follows:

TWO SERIOUS LADIES, by Jane Auer Bowles. (Borzoi).
Registered in the name of Jane Auer Bowles, under
A 172392 following publication April 19, 1943. No
renewal found.

Search in the Renewal Indexes under the above name and
title failed to disclose any renewal registration
relating to ths entry. (Please refer to Circular R15-
Renewal of Copyright).

Of your remittance, $30.00 has been applied in payment
for this search and report. The unused balance of
$10.00 will be refunded in approximately 12 weeks by
official check under separate cover.

Haunted Houses. For *Cast in Doubt*, I researched Roma, because I was interested in the many Gypsy or Roma on Crete and other places in Greece and, of course, Eastern Europe. What interested me in *Cast in Doubt*, because I was working with the idea of modernism versus postmodernism, was that Gypsies had never wanted a state, a nation, so they were both premodern and postmodern at the same time, which I found fascinating. I did some reading about Roma and read Gypsy folktales, which are amazing. They're all about thieves, stealing the nail from the cross, and so on. These deprecating stories about themselves appear in their folktales. I should read more of them. I was and am interested in thinking about the origins of modernism and the nation-state. And they're a nation but not a state. In the '70s, a Frenchman pushed for a state and it was resisted. It never happened. They're wanderers. They were even meant to be buried standing up. they were even meant to be buried standing up. I like the image, vertical and ready to run. They couldn't run from the Nazis.

I wonder if that idea, and maybe it's a poor analogy, informs how you move through the world as an artist. A feeling of statelessness.

I do feel friendship or acquaintance with different people from different places—all of that is in me. Friends settle in me, they become places I know I can return to. Living in Europe for almost seven years had a tremendous effect. There is a real difference between people who have never left this country to live and others who have. When I returned, my American friends never asked about my time in Europe. I felt a complete disinterest. There was no curiosity, but it was pivotal in my life to understand I was American. You know yourself in relation to other people. You don't know yourself alone in a room. You don't. I would bang up against concepts I took for granted. When I began to think about how my thinking had been shaped . . . That's why I've repeated Kafka's "My education has damaged me in ways I do not even know." It's about de-education, or recognizing your thoughts are not your thoughts.

I'm fascinated by this. I think this idea is what strings all of your work together.

I think that's true. Someone called me an "Agent of Doubt." I hope my memory holds up. I'm not like a lot of writers who keep journals. Once I sit down and start writing, I want to write a book. People are telling me now, "You have to write your memoir." And the truth is I've started, but also the truth is, I know these stories and usually when I write it's about what I don't know. It's boring to write what I know, though it would be the writing that would make the difference. I probably should just talk into my iPhone. You don't want to repeat the stories, again and again. Though writing would be a way to forget them. So, I guess living in Europe started the process of unlearning. I grew up with FDR Democrats. In the 1950s, the idea of communism was terrifying. I had to unlearn and broaden. You become filled with what's around you.

My parents were not racists, but I grew up in a racist system. There's no way a white person in America escapes that. Maybe there's less of it among younger people, but I don't know. Look what America's going through now, the Christian Right, loss of women's rights, voting rights . . . It's paroxysms in reverse, or reverse to what seemed like progress, and now, of course we can't count on progress being progress, because it always indicts itself at some point with its failures. Change isn't progress.

I was talking to someone about contraception and how the birth control pill changed women's lives, and of course men's, but a lot of women my age and younger don't credit its huge benefit, because there were consequences, like getting fucked by guys who you'd never hear from again. But that in the scale of a revolution is nothing. It was

a revolution. Women for millennia were trying to control pregnancies and couldn't. The advent of the pill was like space travel, like going to the moon. It wasn't thought of that way. But it is. And women here might lose that too. Imagine what would happen. We wouldn't be talking about gender. We wouldn't be talking about trans or gender neutrality if women couldn't control their pregnancies.

This advancement opened up possibilities—it really changed everything. I had never thought of it like that.

Yes, exactly. Most people don't.

Technology and Gender

In this interview you said, "People are afraid of change. But I think history is on the side of the trans community, because I think they're part of a wave coming out of feminist theories that is challenging the meaning of the body, what the body stands for, and because you're in this body how it's supposed to act and what it's supposed to look like. It's this great challenge to the idea that the body is the foundation of everything."[2] *What does it mean to be on the right side of history?*

The prison house of gender. As we move into an increasingly technological world, with AI and all sorts of products and concepts, the fixedness of gender, which to me was always a problem—from when I was ten and took on feminism—these have to change. In a poem I wrote when I was eighteen, I wanted to call myself Leo, because I didn't see myself as a woman. I was not fulfilling a woman's duties or roles. I didn't want to have children, though I became pregnant several times. I didn't want to stay home and cook, or be domestic. I didn't want to be a woman or a man. Both demanded conventional roles. I just wanted to be a writer. That would be my life, though there were many obstacles, psychological problems. So, the right side of history—it's a term. A hopeful one, because we don't know. I know many people who now have trans kids and by now some of them are adults. I think it's a harbinger of the future. Being nonbinary. I understand the desire to transform one's self. In Woolf's *Orlando* she handles that beautifully, one is a fluid being. There is a question of essentialism: What is a man? A woman? Man and woman are constructions, so they can be deconstructed.

I think you question that notion a lot.

I've always thought about the problems of gender. It's in my writing in different ways. My subversions, they're rarely mentioned. Anyway in the beginning . . . I think my writing was, for a long time, seen as unsensational. [*laughs*] There's not much said about its rebellious nature. In the collection *This Is Not It*, in a story called "The Undiagnosed," gender is central. No didacticism. I wrote it in 1994, I think.

Becoming

So, this is what I was trying to parse out earlier. It's not the most articulate, but it's close. We move toward or against this authentic or potential self. Recognizing your thoughts are not your thoughts, or possibly your body is not your body, which leads to a greater awareness—a possibility to feel more aligned with whatever this self was meant to be.

That's not my language.

I know.

If I talk only about myself, if I extrapolate from myself into culture or society, let's say, I see that "we" are assigned identities. This is very much in *American Genius, A Comedy*. We live inside those identities, like race—there is no such thing really, a false concept, but people live it on the ground. A person who is Black experiences racism, because of ideas about race; women suffer from debased ideas about women. Women who married before the twentieth century here lost their personhood. They were owned by their husbands. It was a form of slavery and talked about as such in the nineteenth century. Having grown up as a girl, fortunately and unfortunately having had much older sisters, I saw how smart they were, how wrong the attitudes were. And however much I disliked my mother, she was no dope. When I went to college, I was surprised girls thought less of themselves than boys. It was astonishing to me.

That was your family dynamic. That's what you knew.

That's what I knew. I was fortunate. I didn't want to be my sisters, but I recognized they were not these demeaned stereotypes. So, it isn't that I'm moving toward a true self, or a truer self. It's that I continue to recognize there are more possibilities for human existence and how humans might think or live. I think the more you are aware of how others live and think, the more you might question the way you think. I know people who say they like someone's artwork, but only their early work, and I'm thinking, *Why don't you like the later work? What is it about the early work? Where were you in your life?* Or, *What are your previous or fixed concepts of art?* I like to question judgements. I question my own. You have to force yourself to work against your ideas. You can be really wrong about an opinion until you examine it closely, then maybe you'll change your mind. And where did that opinion come from? Or you might not like a work but still find something compelling in it. Likes and dislikes, are these insights? No. And there's that nasty word, "taste." Everyone has it, though many deny it. Taste isn't good or bad. People who think they have good taste are to be avoided. [*laughs*] There's loads of people who wouldn't pick up a book of mine or like one. Fine.

That's why I return to Gertrude Stein's essay, "Composition as Exposition." She's saying, Look, I'm not ahead of my time. It's just that I care deeply about art and writing, and most people don't. She doesn't put those people down. She may have been a total snob, and I'm sure she was, and awful in a lot of ways, but at least in this essay, she understands that the concept of being ahead of your time doesn't hold up, and it's uneven, culture is. I'm involved in writing and thinking, right, and also involved in thinking about others' ideas. Always about history. Predecessors. Today I was thinking about the Middle Ages and how absurd it is that it's called the "Middle Ages" or the "Dark Ages." How do you know you're in the middle of anything? For instance, this could be the Dark Ages. We could be in a dark age.

People would agree.

Yes.

Especially in terms of gender, especially in Indiana.

Around gender?

Yes. The spread of national legislation against health care and representation. I have students grappling with these ideas or choosing to take testosterone.

Hormones are so powerful. Just adding or subtracting a drop of estrogen or testosterone makes you more feminine or masculine. A friend started taking too much T. You could see it in his face, and when he took less his face softened. These masculine, feminine physical attributes are determined by tiny drops. The way we walk and dress are social and cultural attributes, learned ones. Hormones. Knowing this has to affect your thinking about gender.

Definitely, and it's so complicated in terms of where it's coming from, etc. All those things are going to change and shift.

It's part of the great transition we are living in. Transitions can be frightening. And there's the unknown. But what is known can be wrong.

That's the conflict. It's so obvious. The legislation.

Indiana Detour

Indiana is where the Klan started. Did you read Cynthia Carr's book, *Our Town: A Heartland Lynching, a Haunted Town, and the Hidden History of White America*? She found out her grandfather was in the Klan.

My great-great-grandfather was in the Klan.

It's disturbing.

It's hard to understand.

You should read her book.

My grandfather told me this story: During the Great Depression, my great-great-grandfather drove to Chicago right before the banks collapsed and took out all the money for the entire town.

No way. Brilliant. He knew something was going to happen. In other words, the bank was holding securities for them. Wow. How do you do that?

I don't know.

Banking must have been different. Did he have everybody's bankbook?

Good question! It's interesting my grandfather first told my sister, who's biracial and adopted, but never told me until I asked him about it.

He told her about a family member being in the Klan, because she's biracial. A confession?

I don't know. Maybe because my sister posted about Black Lives Matter on Facebook. I think his impulse was to share the family past.

Yes, a sort of confession. So maybe later on if she might've found it, it wouldn't be this buried secret. She's younger than you?

Yes.

And your parents started to adopt after you?

There's an adoption pattern in my family. My mom was adopted, sister was adopted, cousin was adopted. My grandpa and grandma couldn't have kids so they adopted four kids. My mom was also later contacted by her biological parents when she was eighteen, and they've had a relationship since.

Why did the parents have to give her up?

My biological grandma was pregnant in high school and went to a home in the middle of nowhere for the pregnancy, but they later married and had a family. So, they wanted to find her later on. We used to spend a lot of time with that side of the family growing up.

How did your mother feel about this?

Well, now it's complicated, because my grandma has Alzheimer's and my mom's taking care of her. Since that happened, she's really distanced herself from her biological side. I think she's really concentrated on spending time with her mom since these are really the last years. I walked into my grandma's room the other day in memory care and she was just staring at the ceiling in the dark with the TV on, but when I grabbed her attention she recognized my face or the sound of my voice or my smell, because she completely changed. I couldn't understand a word of her demented dialogue, but I knew my presence registered in her mind, body, whatever. It's still so haunting. I often wonder if I'll end up like that. I guess it's natural.

Writing *Mothercare*, I often wondered: *Will I get hydrocephalus?* One day when I'm eighty-seven, I might just lose my mind. David and I have talked about pulling the plug. Not wanting to live like that.

But I wanted to add that Paul Bowles and Harry Mathews affirmed the writing life. I respected them as writers. In a short piece I wrote years ago, after being asked who my influences were, I said Ray Charles. I listened all the time to his records when I was eight. Words and rhythm, words and rhythm.

Jane Bowles

It's a lot easier to meet writers now. MFA programs. Readings. For me, meeting a writer was . . . you know—I didn't get an MFA—it was huge. I met both Paul and Harry through the mail. I didn't meet Paul in person until '87. I saw him a few more times when he came to

America. And I did a really stupid thing. Paul's music was playing at Lincoln Center. I went with Charles Henri Ford and Gregg Bordowitz. By then, Paul was in a wheelchair. I brought Charles over to see Paul. Charles was still walking okay. They hadn't seen each other in fifty years. I don't know what I was thinking, making history or something like that. I regret it. They probably disliked each other. But the writer who had the most influence on me was Jane Bowles. I mean, she directly influenced me, not in writing style. No one can write like her, but when I read *Two Serious Ladies* in Amsterdam, I was astounded.

How old were you?

I was in my twenties. She was writing about girls and women in a unique way. Even though I read Woolf, it was like . . . she didn't write about girls. Bowles made the subject open to me. I could write seriously, experimental, unusual, nontraditional novels, and have girls be the protagonists. That was the beginning of my thinking of *Haunted Houses*, and, before that, of course, *Weird Fucks*. Writing seriously about girls . . . the life of boys was always taken seriously.

What do you think of Carson McCullers?

Oh, I love *The Ballad of the Sad Café*. I often think about that bar scene. I love bars. I do have things happen in bars, and it's not because of McCullers, but reading McCullers and her interesting world of "freaks"...I loved it. I think divisions, like Southern writers . . . I don't think it serves writers well.

Why do you think so?

It's as if Carson McCullers, Flannery O'Connor, Tennessee Williams, even Faulkner, but less so because he made it as a mainstream modernist writer, are not American writers and in that mix. Black, women, gay writers—they are separated from the rest of American writing. "The Best Black Writers" rather than "The Best Writers of Their Generation." Themes can be different, sure, all of that, but writing as writing? A great novel is *The Known World* by Edward P. Jones, a great writer who is Black. I never see his novel or short stories compared with those of white writers. He grew up in D.C. He might be considered Southern.

It's certainly a problem.

Contextual Differences

We can notice regional differences, but Flannery O'Connor as a Southern writer? She's part of American writing. I don't want to think of her only as a Southern writer. It's surprising she was in the first MFA class at Iowa.

I do see how it is limiting, but also it is important to understand the regional differences. You grew up on Long Island. I grew up in Indiana. That is where we're writing from, to a degree.

Yes, but it's more what are the cultural influences at home. What are we seeing, hearing about. What did you read, what movies, games . . . My mother was born on the Lower East Side. My father in Brooklyn. They were poor. First generation. I grew up in Woodmere, Long Island. Suburbia. Middle- and upper-middle class. I rejected it when I realized the limits of my surroundings. When we first moved there, it was much more rural. There was a swamp on my street. There were only three houses. It was called Forest Avenue. The swamp would freeze over in the winter, and we'd go ice skating on it. Now, it's completely built up.

I grew up in the middle of nowhere. My backyard was a corn field.

No!

Yes. In the middle of nowhere. My dad was a pastor. My mom was a kindergarten teacher. They met in Chicago at a church. My dad's first assignment was in Indiana. That was my childhood then I moved to the suburbs. From a rural environment to the suburbs . . .

How old were you?

Seventh grade.

Very potent age. Eleven to twelve.

I always had this romantic view of living in a rural area.

Did you love it when you were a kid?

Oh, I loved it.

You had friends?

Yes.

I guess it could be idyllic.

It was at that age. If I went back now, it wouldn't be the same. I tried, but it obviously cannot ever be the same.

Reading as Analysis

This does go back to the regional conversation.

It also connects to what you said earlier about what we know about ourselves is in relation to others.

We're in conversation. We're relating and responding to each other, and now we know more about each other, but also about ourselves as we respond. That's what analysis is about.

Is that what we're doing when we're reading a novel? Investing in another consciousness.

Yes, I think so. That's part of why people don't want to read novels. The modernists liked to read detective stories. I loved noir writers, like Horace McCoy. But reading a novel asks you to shift your environment. Reading another consciousness challenges you, although the word "challenge" bothers me. If you read a novel, and it's a good one, i.e., my point of view engages you in something other than just a story, but also in its ideas, and the way the story has been written, the language, you do enter a different world. If you read Edith Wharton, whom I love, or Jane Bowles, or James Baldwin, there's another world. A lot of people don't want to give up their worlds. They want their worlds affirmed.

That's hard to understand people who don't want to understand. My mom's like that. She doesn't want to step into another world.

I understand it, I think. Some people who grew up during World War II still hate the Germans and the Japanese. Visceral hatred. I watched Dutch people give German drivers wrong directions—it's called "living memory." Theodor Adorno's essay "Coming to Terms with the Past," translated into English after he was dead, is illuminating and seminally important. He wrote about antisemitism in Germany, but his theories work generally for social or cultural hatreds. Sometime after the war, not sure when, "friendship" groups for Jews and Germans were set up to reduce antisemitism. Adorno wrote that antisemitism had nothing to do with actual Jewish people, but that it resided in the Germans. He was speaking psychoanalytically. Not "You're okay, I'm okay." That's something very hard for many people to understand. The imaginary, projections, etc. Stereotypes hold only because anything negative will confirm a stereotype in the eyes of a prejudiced person. People build their identities around learned ideas, concepts, likes, hates, and don't want to change. They lose their sense of themselves—who they think they are.

III. Reality & Abstraction

Historical Repetition ○ Paralyzed Progression ○ Stephen Shore's Warhol ○ Interview as Novel ○ Synthesized Viewpoint ○ Dreamland ○ John Cale (Sunday Morning) ○ Visual Text ○ Ozu ○ Blank Page ○ Remembrance ○ Madame Realism

Taylor Lewandowski: *The first issue of* The Whitney Review of New Writing *just came in the mail. I was reading the interview with Ishmael Reed while waiting for you. He talks about Langston Hughes and Zora Neale Hurston collecting these anthropological stories about magic. I'm often thinking about this in terms of Hurston, because I'm always teaching her novel* Their Eyes Were Watching God. *We discuss how she mimics Black American speech in the South, especially Florida, and the importance of Hurston as an anthropologist. So I'm wondering, what does it mean to have a cultural memory? How is it sustained or eroded over time?*

Lynne Tillman: I haven't read his interview yet. I should. Not long ago, in an interview, he dissed James Baldwin. Chalking up his career to charming the white establishment. Jealous, bitter? There are many cultures, subcultures. Why is one dominant? First of all, I want to say Hurston wasn't mimicking. She was transcribing, recording. She was writing down what she heard. I would not use the word "mimic."

Oh, yes. Mimic is not the right word.

Historical Repetition

That's a very big question and goes to the heart of a lot of issues I do think about, because memorialization can be wrongheaded and not effective. Different cultures pass on objects or events that were important to them and continue to be important for future generations. Great events, and I mean great in the sense of profound, massive, like slavery in America. Some Americans, white Americans, Black Americans, of course, know that slavery was part of the Constitution—enslaved men would be considered three-fifths of a person, in terms of a census. In that slavery is remembered, it must be understood as a factor in the lives of Americans now, for Black Americans, and, of course, white Americans who need to confront their prejudice. Their, our, racism. We are born into a racialized society. I didn't know it when I was little, because you take for granted your early surroundings. You might notice something. I was aware that a woman, a maid my mother hired, Eliza, was Black. It felt weird, but I didn't know why. Hopefully, you grow to see what you swallowed. You begin to learn about injustice.

You ask is it important to remember and who is remembering. I'm thinking of the Holocaust. People, not only Jewish people, especially in Europe, I would imagine, especially in Germany, are afraid this travesty, this horror in Western society, will be forgotten. There's the McCarthy period. The Vietnam War, assassinations of left-wing leaders in other countries. The murders of Civil Rights leaders, assassinations here. How many people think about the First World War? I know the English still do, they commemorated its one hundred year start in 2014. So many of their men were killed, decimating their population. It might have been part of Neville Chamberlain's thinking when he sought appeasement—the horror of the Great War. The truism, "If you know history, you won't repeat it." I think that's not true. There are psychological forces that are about repetition, returning to an event, a moment, and repeating and repeating. Traumas.

Could you say that again?

Yes. Psychological dynamics that have people repeating the same thing. One pop definition of neurosis, not Freud's, but one definition is repeating the same things and expecting a different result. Repetition when something occurs that awakens a trauma. PTSD, for example. There have been wars and wars, there is rarely peace if ever, and never peace everywhere, then a war against wars, but obviously wars go on. The desire for power, territory . . . I've lived longer than you. What would be important for you to know? I am a representative of people born at a certain time. But not everyone in a generation has the same experiences or responses, obviously. So what is important for you to know? I see changes in language, words that didn't exist before. New things need new words. New attitudes. Which statues should be destroyed, what designations for groups and people should go. Basic, significant social and cultural change in words. Words not being used anymore. Earlier writers, Jane Austen, Nathaniel Hawthorne, used language not used now. The English language is richer than how we use it now. I want to use words that aren't necessarily popular. I like the different resonances. Every word has a denotation and intonations. It's wonderful to use those words. Thinking must narrow with a limited vocabulary. I can't prove that. Anyway, new words are always being added. There are changes in style. In the 1940s, going into New York City, everyone dressed formally. Look at Rudy Burckhardt's films and photographs. People wore hats, dresses. Now we wear anything. There have been vital changes, I'm talking about the US, in terms of race and voting, rights of women, workers, and on, but that's part of why there's been such furious kickback, the rise of the Right. Along with a very conservative—I'd call hateful—Supreme Court. But returning to memorialize: What is it that you fear you're losing? What is it that you want to keep? How do we keep these things without idealizing them? For instance, the '60s, idealized, the '80s and Downtown New York.

What do you think?

My impulse is to think about the act of memorializing and trying to preserve images, voices for the formation of identity to come. So, I see this idea also connected to the vocation of the writer, this impulse, which I'd assume at its grandest level breaks down those psychological forces. It seems to me the book stands the test of time, even though it is an object that will decay.

Paralyzed Progression

It's a great technology. It's portable. Easy to use. It has lasted since Gutenberg's Bible. And now on Kindle. When radio came in—I was doing research for *Bookstore*—there was worry that people wouldn't read books anymore. There have always been people who read so-called "literary" books and books that are not "literary." There's a mix. It's not one cultural class. Writing on the Internet produces another way of reading. I'm used to reading on the page. I do read things online. I wouldn't read a novel that way, but short articles, yes. Even Harry Mathews, when I emailed him some short piece of mine, read it on the screen. [*laughs*] But you read differently. The effect of scrolling, whether you're going up and down or left and right, has a different impact on how you read. Of course, scrolls are an ancient form. People were afraid, when personal computers arrived, they'd make writers sloppy, but because I'm a terrible typist, it made me super rigorous. I could immediately change something. The culture around books changes. How we write changes and words we use change. What I thought, recently, Taylor, is that human beings have changed so little in comparison to technology.

Yikes.

We think from the telephone to the electric light to iPhones and all of these gadgets that it means humanity has changed, progressed, but I doubt it. We have more ways to communicate, but how different are humans from those in the Renaissance or eighteenth-century France?

You're arguing humanity has not changed.

I would say, given the cruelty that exists in every generation, over history, every place, more or less, no, we're not so different. In this country, so violent, so terrible, it makes you feel that we are out of control. As if there's no way to reason with other people or discuss things to find a solution, or just understanding, without using a gun. People don't hear each other, they talk over them, they want to be heard. We copy sound bites. We just react. It's terrible. I don't think we can credit the human race with a whole lot except inventions.

Stephen Shore's Warhol

In both The Velvet Years *and* Bookstore: The Life and Times of Jeannette Watson and Books & Co. *you memorialize two specific histories of New York City. How did* The Velvet Years *come about?*

It was 1993, my first year teaching at Bard in their MFA program. *Cast in Doubt* had just come out. I was loose in terms of what I was going to write. That summer The Velvet Underground regrouped, and they played England for the first time. It may have been the first time they played outside America, so pictures by Stephen Shore began to show up in magazines. The Velvet Underground were a great sensation, because no one had seen them live but listened to them all these years. Stephen received a phone call from Pavilion Books. They wanted him to do a book on the Velvets. He said I'll do a book of my Factory photographs, which he had never shown. He made those when he was seventeen to nineteen. In a way, he had forgotten about them, such early work. A couple weeks before he was called by Pavilion, I had gone up to him and said, "I was at a party at your parents' apartment" . . . with some friends, Warhol people, the Velvets. I had remembered him standing in front of a bay window that looked out at the East River—a fancy neighborhood in Manhattan. He was standing there, looking very shy, diffident, with his arms akimbo. I had a perfect picture of him watching this scene.

So, when he was asked by Pavilion to do this, they asked him, "Who would you want to write it?" He said, "Lynne Tillman." They said fine. I had a couple of books published in London. Of course, to no acclaim, but I guess they knew about them or me. So Stephen called me and asked if I wanted to do this. I said sure. But Stephen had never read anything I wrote. He thought, he told me later, that because I was teaching at Bard's MFA program, I must be a good writer. He took a chance. We started meeting, I taped him talking about the Factory. He had made copies of his photographs, and, of course, all of the photographs were black-and-white. There were over two hundred. He asked me if I could make a book out of this. I had never designed a book before, conceptualized one like this. I thought about how to do it. I talked with the artist Barbara Bloom, who knew what to consider. *I'm not going to write a research book*, I decided. I'm not going to write my opinions of the Factory and the people involved, but most of his pictures were of people, so I interviewed as many as I could find.

I wanted to see the people as interesting, not just hangers-on, not clones of Andy, or negligible. It wasn't true they were only that. Some were not in good shape then, Pope Ondine, for one. But many were. Because I had hung out at Max's Kansas City in college, I had become friends with some of them, like Donald Lyons and Danny Fields. I interviewed eighteen people, dropped myself out of the conversations,

THE VELVET YEARS: WARHOL'S FACTORY 1965-67
Photographs by Stephen Shore. Text by Lynne Tillman.
Published by Thunder's Mouth Press. Pub. Date: February 27, 1996
ISBN 1-56025-098-4
Press Contact: Ira Silverberg Communications 212-741-8500

THE VELVET YEARS: WARHOL'S FACTORY 1965-67
Photographs by Stephen Shore. Text by Lynne Tillman.
Published by Thunder's Mouth Press. Pub. Date: February 27, 1996
ISBN 1-56025-098-4
Press Contact: Ira Silverberg Communications 212-741-8500

and turned the interviews into prose narratives. I thought of what I was making as a novel of pictures and words. In terms of layout I wanted the pictures, which I learned was a little unusual, on the left hand side, so that when you would turn a page the text would be on the right side. Each person or character had their own chapter in this novel. I was given 30,000 words, and left 2,500 for my introductory essay on Warhol, "Like Rockets and Television."

That was my first work on Warhol. Years later, in the early 2000s, I did another conversation with Stephen for his book *Uncommon Places: The Complete Works*. My first question was about Andy Warhol's influence on him. It turned out I was the first writer to suggest Warhol's influence on him. That was clear to me, particularly in his early work, *American Surfaces*. His use of snapshots was influenced by Warhol's attitude toward art and the vernacular. Nobody had known his Factory work. They talked about Walker Evans and other great photographers, who, of course, were an influence on Stephen, but his projects, his ideas were affected by a Warholian sensibility.

Interview as Novel

You also used this approach to string together the interview as a sort of chorus-like novel in Bookstore.

I used the same technique. I interviewed Jeannette Watson about twenty times. Her memory was not great, but talking with her loosened more stories. I interviewed, I don't know, many other people, who had something to do with Books & Co. I decided to make Jeannette the narrator, and I would use other people's thoughts to interrupt her flow. For instance, when she mentioned her father, I used a quote from Brendan Gill about him that augmented her story, but we'd always return to her narrative. It took me nearly three years to do this. It was supposed to be a project like *The Velvet Years*, which took about eight months of my time, but *Bookstore* ended up taking three years because when I signed on for *Bookstore*, it was to write portraits of people who used the bookstore, but after I signed the contract, a month later, I found out the bookstore was closing. Without Jeannette saying anything to me, and because I'm a lunatic and must finish and do a great job, rather than breaking the contract and saying I couldn't do it now, I knew I had to write a cultural and social history. That's why there's an index and every reading ever given is listed. I had Rone Shavers research that. There was no list before. Some people really enjoy the book. It also has insight into the publishing world at that moment.

Oh, yeah. Both of these books are so wonderful and important. It's odd neither of these are referenced or talked about much in relation to your other writing. They fit into your preoccupations with perception, especially Bookstore, *taking on Jeannette's perspective and formulating it into a novelistic structure.*

Synthesized Viewpoint

People would say, "You're writing a book about a bookstore, how boring is that!" Someone said that to me, casually, like saying your lover is a shit or stupid. I was determined to make it interesting. I went into it as a concept. I didn't know how a bookstore operated. I didn't know why certain books were there or not. I'm not talking about a Barnes & Noble, which was very popular at the time. I'm talking about independent bookstores, because as a kid you go into a bookstore and think every book in the world is going to be there. Books & Co. had an amazing buyer named Peter Philbrook. It was his taste—to use that word—his education, his culture. It was a curated space. He controlled what was on the center table. As soon as you walked in, there was a long, oblong table with new books. It was like being in a candy store. You wanted to consume all of them, really—to continue that metaphor. It was amazing. You went to Books & Co. to see what was out. But my bookstore was St. Mark's, which was in my neighborhood, and it was a great bookstore. I didn't go to Books & Co. much, but I did whenever I was at the Whitney Museum or if I was meeting someone from *Art in America*, like my friend Craig Owens. I learned how they operated from the salespeople, publishers, buyers. I knew nothing. I thought readers or people interested in books would also be interested in this. I utilized my ignorance.

It is a beautiful cultural history and another argument for the importance of independent bookstores. I want to return to Andy Warhol. How has he influenced you?

Dreamland

He's very important to me. When I saw his work as a young teenager, it hit me like a rocket, or, as he would say, like rockets and television. I was stunned by it. It made a lot of sense to me. I don't know if that clarifies anything. What he was doing upended my expectations, looking at the tomato soup cans and thinking about the everyday that seems so forgettable and unimportant. And then seeing those early car crash pieces, which was also a part of daily life. Or the electric chair as a foreboding object that arrived with electricity, with progress. Now, we can electrocute people. [*laughs*] I read *Delirious New York*, Rem Koolhaas's book about the amazing project that was Coney Island and its use of electricity—to electrify an elephant. Painful to see. I did see it in a doc made about Coney Island. It was incredibly disturbing. In the same film, I also saw Freud walking into Dreamland. He came to New York in 1909. I had just published an essay in *Art in America* called "Freud in Dreamland," and I didn't know that he had in fact visited Dreamland. I knew he'd gone to Coney Island, and he had said it was the place he liked best in America. I just imagined he'd go to Dreamland; the film documented that he did. Warhol's work was about reality and abstraction. His great ability to put things in an art gallery, like his silver balloons, which were really silly and provocative, like Duchamp. Of course, his films were fascinating. It opened a different window for looking and thinking about art.

What year did you first see a Warhol?

Must have been early '60s. '63 or '64. I didn't go to his early shows, but I saw pictures of pictures. I don't know when I saw his work in galleries. I'm not sure, but I do remember the pictures.

John Cale (Sunday Morning)

Is this around the time you met John Cale?

It's somewhat after. I think I met John when I was nineteen or twenty. I don't remember exactly who introduced us or how, but I had a good friend, Hope Ruff (that was really her last name), a singer and musician. She was hanging out with Warhol people. She was some years older. We shared an apartment in the East Village, and we both attended Hunter. She invited me to parties or whatever. Maybe I met John at the Exploding Plastic Inevitable. I don't remember. All I remember, once I was his "girlfriend," I went with him one afternoon to The Dom, and Nico was sitting on the stairs, and they said hello. I didn't know she had been his last girlfriend. It was so odd. She was an icon, this ice queen. John and I hung out for about a year. We had sex for a much shorter amount of time. I don't know if John was doing drugs then or not. Maybe he was, because his visits to me or my meetings with him became less frequent, but I was determined to maintain a relationship years after. He was one of the first artists in my life. Someone who devoted himself. Not that he was the model artist, I should say. [*laughs*]

So, what's this story about John Cale and "Sunday Morning"?

I remember hanging out with John and Lou Reed only twice. The first time Lou was so nasty to me that I developed the runs. [*laughs*] Later John told me he had told Lou, "You cannot treat my girlfriend like that." This was early in our relationship. The next time I remember being with Lou and John, it must have been very late, 3:00 a.m., and I don't remember where we were beforehand, or if we were anywhere beforehand. We met up with Lou and went to an after-hours gay club. All men. It was like Prohibition times, illegal, and you had to show your face through a peephole before you were let in, because, of course, homosexuality itself was illegal. It was terrible and crazy. It was my second time with "illegal" men. I had been taken to a party . . . I wonder if "gay" was used then, I don't think so. This is '65 I think, so different from now—thankfully. I had a close friend, Al, who was gay and so smart and so much fun and crazy. I thought of feminism and gay liberation as the same thing. Anyway, he took me to the party. It was on Park Avenue across the street from the church where Norman Vincent Peale used to preach. All men, all in suits dancing. Some old fashioned 8 mm porn on a screen. I'm the only girl, the only female there of any kind. It was a formal party in a way. Al should not have brought me. My presence was not wanted. The host was a sweet guy. He saw that I was uncomfortable. I was a college girl. I didn't know what to do. If I should sit down or stand up or leave. My friend suddenly disappeared. He had greener pastures. He was not in a suit. He was a young guy. The men looked like they were all in their thirties or forties. The porn looked homemade, not the porn of today. I decided to leave. The host saw me walk toward the door. He was sweet. He opened the door and said, "Why don't we get together some time for some good, clean fun?" [*laughs*] I think he was embarrassed that such a young girl was there. I don't know. We may have hugged. That was the first time I saw men in suits dancing with each other. I was on the outskirts of the Warhol crowd. I would go to Max's. And by the time I knew John, I was used to being with gay men, but not in suits. [*laughs*] It must be hard for a twenty-five-year old now to imagine how gay people had to hide to dance together. Terrible.

That is a striking image.

It was very striking. Oh, there was a guy. I think he was the Velvet's bouncer, Saizon. John would remember. A big, muscular guy. He wore a cape, very imposing looking. I assume that's how Lou knew about the gay after-hours club. We walked in and sat down. There were men dancing with men. This was a secret place.

This was the same place?

No. This was in a club, not someone's loft. Entirely different situation. We hung out there for a while. Lou said to John, "Why don't we go to so-and-so's place?" It was a time of going from place to place. Aimlessly. It happened to be on Fifteenth Street off Third Avenue in a modern-looking, white-brick apartment building. Still there. Lou rang the bell. I was thinking, *It's three in the morning. What are we doing?* A guy answered and we went up. It wasn't weird showing up at this place at this hour. I think a woman was there too. There was a piano against a wall. It was an old-fashioned, upright piano. John sat down at the piano. Something about Sunday morning, which it was. Early Sunday morning, three or four in the morning. He started humming, singing, "Sunday morning, Sunday morning." Playing chords. That's what I remember. It was very fitting. It had a bluesy, in-the-middle-of-the-night lonely feel. A sort of lonely song.

Wow. Yeah.

I briefly wondered back then if he and Lou ever had sex. Lou was bisexual, or ambisexual, but no, John is very heterosexual.

Visual Text

You are and have been connected to the art world. There's a strong connection between friends, colleagues, or both. Artists like Barbara Kruger, Laurie Simmons, Cindy Sherman, Louise Lawler, Susan Hiller, Robert Gober and others.

Lots of artists. I'm on the periphery as a writer.

Stephen Prina.

Yes. Wonderful artist and friend. I met him in LA with Chris Williams. I can't cite everyone. I have many close friendships that are dear to me. Maybe one day I'll write my version of Aubrey's *Brief Lives*. [*laughs*] And I've been very fortunate to be around this world, this art world, to have close artist friends, and to be asked to write for artists.

The commonalities among these artists, especially Kruger, Simmons, and Sherman, and ideas around representation, identity, deconstructing the American Dream, objects in context, or taking them out of a context.

I felt I understood what they were doing, felt for it, almost viscerally. It felt right. Like Warhol's art, their work made sense to me. Since I was young, I've been interested in art. First, movies. I was often taken to movies by my sisters on a Saturday to keep me quiet. This was before cable. But there was TV. I watched a lot, I read books with one eye on the screen. Eventually I got into the history of cinema and, like everyone, wanted to make a film, but more than anything I wanted to write. And much later did, with Sheila McLaughlin, *Committed*, a feature-length film based on actor Frances Farmer's life, that came out in 1984 at the Berlin Film Festival. It was a feminist narrative film, not a documentary.

As a kid, I would take out the projector and watch my family's 8 mm films by myself. My father made most of the movies before I was born and some after. I was trying to figure out the world before Lynne. My father was a textile designer and manufacturer. He was interested in the feel and color of these fabrics. I remember the bolts of material.

My middle sister was a ballet dancer. She took me to the ballet when I was very little. I was inducted into these different arts and crafts. I used to draw until the second grade. I was apparently the best artist in class in first grade until a new girl joined the class. Her name was Jane Hope Greenberg. I've never forgotten it. She became the best artist in class. She had art lessons; she knew perspective. I gave up art. I stopped trying to be an artist. Years later, I had a friend in high school who encouraged me to draw. I made a charcoal drawing of my dog, Lady. In college, I took all my electives in studio art. I'd go to MoMA, the Met, see some shows, no regularity. Then I left for Europe and got into experimental film. I had different interests. When I returned to New York after living in Europe, I gravitated to visual artists. I was terrified of actual writers. I was so insecure, Taylor.

You felt more comfortable around visual artists?

Oh, yes. Much more comfortable. Early on, I showed Kathy Acker a very short piece I wrote. She was basically dismissive. It was a great

DUTCH FILM MAKERS COOP

Jos Schoffelen will be present to introduce and discuss films by:

Lynne Tillman
Barbara Meter
Mattijn Seip
Niko Paape
Tom Chomont
Jos Schoffelen
Peter Erdmann
Kurt Kren

Wednesday, February 12, 8:30pm
Museum of Art Theatre
Film Section, Information: 622-3212
Museum of Art, Carnegie Institute
Admission $1.00

struggle to show my writing or allow myself to write. I went into psychoanalytic psychotherapy again. In college, it kept me from offing myself. I was very depressed. When I lived in Europe, I visited New York and my family only twice. My parents came to Paris one time. I met them with my oldest sister. We were in a restaurant and Simone de Beauvoir was there. I remember we had an argument. Everybody always argued in my family. It was a nightmare. I was so humiliated. What if Simone de Beauvoir heard us? [*laughs*] It was entirely humiliating. Because I started a cinema in Amsterdam, when I came back to New York City I had some recognition from filmmakers.

You started a cinema?

Yes, with my partner at the time, Jos Schoffelen. It's a city with lots of artists—the government supported the arts well. That's changed now, and throughout Europe, there's less money for the arts. Of course, there's little here, almost nothing. Theaters were not showing interesting films in Amsterdam, usually second-rate or new mainstream films, so we started a cinema. We called it the Electric Cinema, based on the Electric Cinema in London. We rented nights in a disused movie theater from the owner, Mr. Goedings. Thursday to Sunday nights, and showed double features, which was the first time in Amsterdam that happened. So in itself that was something.

In order for us to rent movies, we had to be a film club. This distinguished us from commercial theaters and didn't compete with them. It took a minimal amount of money to rent films from the Film Museum in Amsterdam. In one night, we showed both parts of Sergei Eisenstein's *Ivan The Terrible*, I and II. In Dutch, it was *Ivan de verschrikkelijke*, which was hard to say over the phone. [*laughs*] We ran the cinema for a couple of months, but it didn't last after Jos and I broke up. But before that we had gotten in a lot of trouble, because I carried back an illegal print of Warhol's *Bike Boy* from London in my suitcase. We rented it from a guy who should not have rented it to us.

No Warhol film had ever been shown in Amsterdam. This was 1970. Never. We got in a lot of trouble because we advertised that we were showing it. The movie theater mafia was infuriated. They wanted to shut us down. The film museum took away our membership so we couldn't rent their films anymore. I don't know if it will ever be historically noted, but we were the first people to show *Bike Boy* in Amsterdam.

So, I had some recognition among film people, like Jonas Mekas. Our cinema had an amazing audience for experimental films, which most people had never seen. We'd sell out the theater for a structural film. They were hungry for something new. Malcolm Le Grice showed a film called *Castle One (The Light Bulb Film)*, and people sat in the dark for a while and suddenly a very powerful lightbulb lit up the entire theater. Boom. And that was it. It was kind of great. Film is important to me. When I got back from Europe, I met Amy Taubin, who was then making films, a brilliant film critic and teacher—we became friends.

I met Martha Wilson, who was just starting Franklin Furnace. I remember a meeting in 1978 to see if the Furnace could provide artists who were not employed by Franklin Furnace with health insurance. I was there and so was Barbara Kruger. I think she sat in front of me. Something she said or her laugh made me want to be friends with her. It was the beginning of our long friendship. I kept meeting artists. But these three women were there at the very beginning.

Which brings me back to your comments about when I returned to New York and how the work of different artists affected me. I didn't answer, really, and went into my history, instead. So, for instance, the Pictures Generation people you cited. And others. Their approach to representation, decoding cultural objects, analyzing what is often taken for granted, how pictures needed to be read critically.

Images and their power, the ways people identify with images, or choose their images—their work profoundly affected me, as well as the writing on their work, and I found ways to see that work in relation to writing. It gave me ideas. And like Warhol, their work, as I said, made sense to me visually, intellectually, psychologically.

There were many loft parties in the late '70s into the '80s. It was easy to meet people, anyway it was for me then. And still. My significant other, bass player supreme, David Hofstra—he says insignificant other—was playing with a number of punk bands and jazz bands. In the late '70s early '80s. Bob Musial, Phillip Johnston, James Chance, Rashid Ali, John Zorn, Elliot Sharp, Jody Harris, and more. David played on critic Lester Bangs's only record, and in his band at its only gig at CBGB. I already knew artist Barbara Ess, who had a punk band, Y Pants. I gave Y Pants lyrics for a song, "Do the Obvious." Things or life expanded. New York excited me, the people did. I had lived in a very small part of London. My art world centered around Susan Hiller, Barbara Ess, Carla Liss, and the London Film-Makers' Co-op. North London. A bit later I became friends with Heathcote Williams, the playwright, and his partner Diana Senior, and their daughter China. They had squatted in a house in Ladbroke Grove, and I lived there. I recall I directed an odd variety show Heathcote put on at the Royal Court theater. It got out of hand, uncontrollable. In the booth, I gave up. [*laughs*]

I became very close with Susan Hiller. She may have been the most significant person for me as a writer and artist—the most encouraging, the most interested in my becoming a writer, getting rid of my obstacles. She paid attention. Susan was a brilliant artist, writer, thinker, reader. She read everything. Her knowledge was extensive. Her questions, comments, insights. She was an independent thinker and resisted groupthink, didn't go along with intellectual trends, was anarchic in her thinking, and that didn't stand well in some circles. Also, she was an American in London; her husband, David Coxhead,

a writer, was English. They went to live in London in 1965 or 1966. I think her being an American, a woman, and Jewish—let's never forget baked-in English anti-Semitism—was an issue. Her training in anthropology led her to think about culture and art differently. Susan worked with and against belief systems. In various media, in linguistics, also. Too much to say, really.

One of her near-to-last pieces was a film about disappearing languages, with voices speaking those disappearing or extinct languages, the words and meanings on the screen. Amazing. Who else would have done this? Our one big argument was about Freud and dreams. She read Freud, thought he was brilliant, of course, important, but she didn't think that his theory of dreams was the only one that was right. We argued, then she said let's stop because we weren't going to change each other's opinion. But, and this was crucial, Susan made me very aware that it was my belief system. It might not be absolutely right but in a sense right for me. Intelligent people I know, some thought she believed in auras, ghosts. She was interested and respected people who believed differently, in otherworldly and irrational events. The irrational in a sense was her field, a part of human life. She didn't observe the sanctities. She wanted to undo some. She died in 2019. I miss her so much . . .

Anyway, back in London I had very long, very full hair. I was known for this, I suppose. This is funny. An actor, a woman playing a New Yorker, apparently wore a big, black wig to play a New York woman. Anyway, in New York I felt comfortable around visual artists and filmmakers. Then I met Gary Indiana, Patrick McGrath, Catharine Texier, Joel Rose, Ted Castle. So I began to meet writers like myself who were not published. When our books came out, they called us "Downtown Writers," and that label has stuck. Very annoying to me. Patrick McGrath quickly broke out when he published *The Grotesque.* Betsy Sussler started *BOMB* Magazine, and soon I published something in it, under my name. Gary Indiana and I became close. We shared a sense of the absurd, the morbid in politics and in writing and writers, and we still mostly love each other's work. Conversations with Gary range wildly, and we end up laughing. We once laughed for thirty minutes about the first sentence of someone's book. No names.

You dedicated No Lease on Life *to Gary, and he dedicated* Rent Boy *to you, right?*

It seemed perfect that *No Lease on Life* was dedicated to him. I didn't think twice. Also, all the jokes, he loved that. When it came out, Gary said something to me like, now I can't do that. There was some competition, but it was not vicious, the healthy kind, I think, if that really exists. Prosaically, Gary and I shared the bars, galleries, streets, nights, grocery stores, and lived on the same blocks for more than half our lives. The neighborhood has changed, of course, but neither of us felt it was completely ruined, though he might have more complaints than I. It was a little awkward his dedicating *Rent Boy* to me, because in it, a character is based on Kathy Acker, and it wasn't complimentary. I didn't say anything to him, though. There was no point. That's the thing about something going into print. Not long ago, Gary apologized for using a story I had told him to end *Horse Crazy*. It was my story, and I was upset, really shocked. So not long ago, I used it in a story I wrote. Then I read Nate Lippens's Instagram about telling that story as if it was his, because he didn't know where he'd read it. I told Gary, and we roared with laughter. I wrote Nate that it was fine, and now he knows the whole story of the story.

I had no clue. I remember Nate mentioning it on his Instagram. Like Gary and these writers who have been labeled "Downtown Writers," I wonder if there is any value bunching them together, certainly you and Gary do share affinities. You both share a type of cynicism but also sensitivity, reverence, energy to write against a world steeped in violence. I recently read this interview with Ariana Reines, which attempts to scratch at the idea of language or literature as a transformative act. It also aligns with David Rattray's concepts. She even calls it "writing what's invisible, or apparently invisible." She says, "I've been haunted by the old mode of writing, which I think of as 'righting' —seeking redemption, somehow, by rendering past events into art; into fiction, into vision, into some form of intellectual lucidity that could somehow free me from the shit of the real. This is how the old dudes used to do it, and it's not without its value. But what fascinates me is writing's relationship to the future. Every book I've written has radically transformed my life. It has materially altered my lifestyle, brought me into contact with new friends and lovers, artworks and countries, ideas and vibrations I had neither the guts nor the imagination to visualise in advance."³ So, I'm connecting this to your own writing in relation to writers, like Gary and others, as Ariana's own books "altered" her life. Regardless of how we denigrate the book, it is an object that does have serious consequences on our own lives once it's out in the world. Returning to those earlier days before you published anything, I assume you first found connection, encouragement among visual artists, which at first I found surprising, but it isn't considering your time at Hunter.

First, I have to say, I don't denigrate books. I denigrate bad writers. [*laughs*] How people respond to my books doesn't change me. Though I have learned from some responses to my books that I wouldn't have imagined. For instance, if you don't say a woman is beautiful, then she must not be. I don't feel, as Ariana does, that each book I wrote altered my life. No. Actually what does change a life? Meeting a person? I know that living in Europe for almost seven years changed my life. Analysis has. Different deaths I've experienced. Yes, I received encouragement from artists, but it's not clear cut. When I first knew the art world, it was the New York art world, not a global scene the way it is now.

I've been watching foreign films since I was a teenager. Books, of course, reading in translation. First, Thomas Mann. Film always struck me as international. And it was available. Agnes Varda, Fassbinder, Peter Greenaway, Godard, Truffaut, Fellini, Antonioni, spaghetti westerns, at least I was into them, and on and on. I knew about European experimental film, because of having lived there and screened those films—the Heins, Birgit Hein especially, Valie Export, Peter Kubelka, Kurt Kren, the disgraced Otto Muehl, Gunter Brus. When I first saw Paul McCarthy's work, I thought of the Austrians right away. In London, Sally Potter, Malcolm LeGrice, Laura Mulvey, Peter Wollen. And in London I saw American experimentalists, I remember especially Paul Sharits. But most people I knew in New York in the '80s and '90s were not interested in experimental film. I began watching Ozu films in the '80s. Now he's my favorite director.

Ozu

Yasujirō Ozu is your favorite director?

Yes, I think so. One of my top favorites. It's him, Chantal Akerman, Hitchcock, Fassbinder, Antonioni, Spielberg, some of Eastwood, a lot of Scorsese, too many. Taiwanese film, when I get to see it. I once watched Buñuel and still think of *The Exterminating Angel* a lot. Ozu has a very special place in my heart. There was just an Ozu festival at Film Forum. I saw three or four I hadn't seen before, one of the last films he made called *An Autumn Afternoon*. Maybe the last. The autumn of these men's lives. The focus is on the men's daughters who take care of them after the men's wives die. It's interesting because it's 1962 and things are changing for women in Japan. Of course, they haven't changed enough for women in Japan, pretty much anywhere, not enough, but you see women not in traditional dress, but in so-called Western clothes. They're secretaries, receptionists, not CEOs, but it was a change.

Like watching Ozu or your first encounter with a Warhol, what are some other significant moments looking at art? Also, in relation to how we become aware of our surroundings or how we gain consciousness and ultimately individuate, how has your concept of art changed over the years?

My father took me to see Eero Saarinen's TWA Flight Center building when it was finished. We drove around the airport a few times. It was the first building I recognized as architecture. I remember going to the Museum of Modern Art on my own for the first time when I was fifteen. I went into the city. The Museum was different then. It was much smaller. It felt personal. It was an absolutely wonderful space. It didn't feel like a supermarket of art. Still, it's amazing, the kind of shows they put on now. I just saw Stuart Comer and Michelle Kuo's exhibition, *Signals: How Video Transformed the World*.

Oh, yeah. I saw that.

Isn't it brilliant?

I was in tears.

Blank Page

Really? It was intriguing that they started the show in 1980. Because it wasn't about television, but about transmissions. The curators did an amazing job. I don't want to knock any of that. It was a very different museum then. I remember seeing a painting. I thought about it a year ago. I remember walking up the stairs, and there was a painting of someone walking up the stairs. Oskar Schlemmer's *Bauhaus Stairway*. Everything seemed important to me. Even though I was a young feminist, I wasn't yet thinking, "Oh there aren't enough women or there

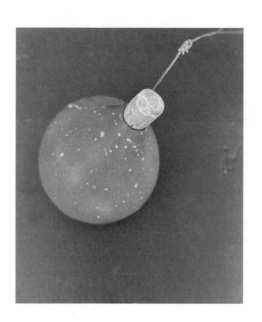

aren't enough Black artists. Why aren't there?" I was a young teenager; I was just stunned by what was there. When I was sixteen, I went to their cinema. They were showing experimental films. There was *Pull My Daisy*, Bruce Connor's *Marilyn*. I was blown away. I had never seen films like these. From then on, I was interested in so-called experimental or underground or independent films. I went back to MoMA many times. Always alone. It was cheaper back then too.

In college, as I mentioned, I was taking all of my electives in studio art and thinking about painting. Gorchov wanted me to get an MFA in art. But I realized that painting, that canvas, that sheet of paper I'd drawn on, was not the blank space I wanted to occupy. Concentrating on it helped me see a way of representing other than words and helped me understand visual art. I felt I was using a different part of my brain. Being aware of spatial relations, color, the edges of the canvas, visual compositions. There's obviously space on a blank page, but it is very different. I think, overall, when I look at art . . . It's really a strange thing, art. Its value and its ephemerality or longevity. And how my thinking developed. You have to be very bold to make art. I've done many studio visits over the years. Many, many, many studio visits. You walk into an artist's studio and it's always a surprise. Sometimes it's a great surprise and sometimes it's not, but you see people trying to work things out visually, conceptually in a different way from writing. What I gained from looking at art, talking about it, and this is more to your question, is a different way of approaching writing. It caused me to think about writing somehow differently, from ellipses to juxtapositions, to what can and can't be done. I find it encouraging and helpful, and because I'm not a visual artist it's not painful to see shows. [*laughs*] The work educates me, encourages my imagination. The concepts often amaze and confound me. I also remember my first visit to the Museum of Natural History. I was a child. What struck me were the large vitrines and the different animals of different eras. It was fascinating what had lived so long ago. It's also art in a sense. But obviously everything you see, read, whatever affects your consciousness, how you live in the world and think about the world, is culture and art.

Remembrance

This also connects to Craig Owens's approach of writing "alongside art" rather than about art. I recently read your conversation with Ross McElwain about Craig Owens.[4] Along with Scott Bryson, Barbara Kruger, and Jane Weinstock, you edited the only collection of Craig Owens's writing, Beyond Recognition: Representation, Power, and Culture. *What was the process of editing this book?*

We began soon after Craig died of AIDS. In his lifetime, he didn't want to publish a collection. Maybe it was insecurity, but also mixed with humility. You have to remember he died at thirty-nine. A lot of the work he produced came out in his twenties. The last essay was in 1987, I think. Before he died, he was staying with his parents outside Chicago. Thinking and writing about Pasolini, Fassbinder, and Almodóvar—three great queer artists. He was a thorough intellectual with a fertile creative mind. Brilliant. He was unique, and I mean one of a kind.

So, we pulled together all the essays and articles he had written. We chose a majority of his published work. We kept the work as is. We didn't reedit. Simon Watney, who was a writer and AIDS activist, which Craig wasn't (an AIDS activist), wrote the introduction. We four discussed the essay, which in the first instance did not meet our expectations. So I wrote him with all our comments, and he sent back a revised, perfectly wonderful essay. Barbara came up with a beautiful design. By working on it, it felt like Craig was alive, but when the book came out, I felt he was really dead. It was an odd feeling, that finality. Books have a life, but they're not the person. The book would go out in the world, but not Craig. He was no longer there.

But in some ways he is, right?

Well, he's in my mind. I keep an object he gave me when he returned from South America. He had traveled with Lothar Baumgarten, whose work he was really interested in in the early '80s. They had gone to the Amazon river together. Craig brought back a clay receptacle with a cork in it. You could carry water in it. It's small, and beautifully handmade. The day of his death was July 4th, 1990. He died at about four in the morning. I remember the phone call from Scott Bryson, who was his boyfriend and also a co-editor of the book. We knew it had to come sooner rather than later. About eight months before he died, he had moved to his parents' place so he could easily use his wheelchair. We spoke on the phone, not a lot, probably twice a month. I had the feeling he didn't want too many calls. Whenever I said, I wanted to fly out, he said, "No, no. I'll feel better next month." He was always delaying it, but finally Jane Weinstock and I had to go to a wedding on the West Coast, so we decided to visit him. We were there for a weekend. Craig was filled with life, full of ideas. We had a spirited conversation. It was awful leaving him. I still remember his expression as we were getting into a taxi, leaving him.

It's awful.

AIDS was a desperate plague, I think worse than Covid because of the stigma attached to gay men and women, and drug users, and lack of government care until Fauci came along, and that was because of ACT UP. He got it. I believe Gregg Bordowitz was part of that group who met with him. Young and older men—gay men—were dying every day. Boom. Fast. Terrifying. Keith Davis was twenty-five, an artist who designed the chapbook *Madame Realism* I did with Kiki Smith. Keith and I met once to talk about the book. This was 1983. The next month he was dead. Deaths, more and more. Funerals, memorials. David Wojnarowicz refused to attend any more memorials. Fran Lebowitz made a trenchant remark: It wasn't just the loss of famous artists, dancers, musicians that was horrific, it was the loss of their audience. I'm paraphrasing. Now it's forty years ago, not that AIDS is over, but two generations ago, and it's very hard to explain what it felt like except to say it devastated a community, ravenously, my community also, and it seemed it would never end. Craig was taken.

In that interview, you also mention meeting Craig with Barbara Kruger on the street and a lunch with him at a steak and burger restaurant on Lexington. How did these conversations influence your own life or how you viewed art?

If you went into Soho in the '80s, before Chelsea had arrived, on a busy art day, Friday or Saturday, you'd bump into people and talk, which was usually passing conversation. When I want to have a serious conversation, I usually want to sit down. Even at parties, where you walk around and say hello. But if it's serious I'll say, "Why don't we sit down?" Because too much buzz is around, too many faces. It's important for me to be able to concentrate. I missed all these conversations during lockdown. While Zoom and the phone helped, seeing the person, their body language, is so important. What's your question? Craig wrote about "writing alongside art." We are alongside it, sometimes in front of it. We aren't making the art, but living in the same time of its making. You're around it, and it may have something to do with your life. I think he wanted to know how and why.

Madame Realism

Owens was really wrestling with postmodernism, so I'm wondering how does this relate to your own work? I see it directly in the Madame Realism stories.

I started and wrote the first Madame Realism story before I knew Craig's work, but his work became very influential to my thinking. His position on postmodernism is different from the way many other critics since him write about it. They see a sort of grab bag, apolitical, not at all how Craig saw it. For him, it was about bringing into art the work of marginalized people. Moving away from Lyotard's "grand narrative" into creating room for other narratives. It was a rebuke to the modernist canon, which included a few women and people of color, but essentially they were excluded. Craig wrote a seminal essay on feminism and postmodernism. He was interested in moving away from canonical modernism, as well as the *October* regime, and don't ask me to explain *October*'s point of view. It was most important in the 1970s and 1980s, but dogmatic and restrictive. By saying writing alongside, I think Craig meant he did not want to be dogmatic, not to judge art as he had but to recognize he was living alongside it, along with it. It's evident in the interview.[5] I think he was moving toward different ideas and rebuking earlier ideas. He followed other people's ideas unwittingly. He said, they were not his ideas. He wanted to find out what he thought, what he could say. To think differently. It's very clear in the interview. Don't you think so?

Yes, definitely.

Have you ever seen the video?

No!

Oh, god. You can go online and see it. You must watch it. It's revelatory. Douglas Crimp put together a show of his art collection and other works and included the video interview. I thought seeing it I'd be very upset, but when I saw it, I felt Craig was talking to me again. I was moved and excited to see him. I walked outside and immediately called Paul Chan, artist and publisher of Badlands Unlimited, and told him he had to publish it. More people must see it, know about it. Paul said he'd send his interns to see it, and they agreed, so it happened.

That's great. So, the first Madame Realism story was before Craig, but most of them were published in Art in America?

Oh, yes. From then on, they published most of them. I wrote *Madame Realism* in 1982, as a retort to surrealism, but it wasn't published until 1984, as a chapbook with Kiki Smith. She made drawings for it, and famously her first drawing of sperm. I met Craig in 1980 or 1981.

I was reading your "The Museum of Hyphenated Americans" this morning, which is all about Ellis Island. It serves as a synthesis of your preoccupations, i.e. American history, doubt in authority, perception, and an inability to know one another.

I visited Ellis Island earlier, before it was rehabbed. You felt the ghosts. It allowed another experience, more raw. It wasn't full of information. It felt shadowed by the past. You could feel, imagine people sitting on those benches. You could walk around, there were no guards. Medical instruments covered in dust still lay on tables. It was creepy.

It reminded me of what we were talking about earlier, in terms of remembering. Why is it so important? Or, is this a flawed assumption?

We live in such curious times—people don't memorize much. I used to know everyone's phone number by heart. Back then, having a good memory was a sort of intelligence. Now, people don't need to remember. You can put it in your phone. They don't have to learn how to multiply. I remember learning Latin, French, and trying to memorize in my first year of high school. I have wondered what happens to conscience if you don't remember. How does a conscience develop without memory?

As much as I'm interested in many kinds of history, and wish I knew more about all kinds, I resist reading a bunch of facts or dates, because it's not as compelling as the interpretations of the events, or the fiction of the events. There is usually no documentation except diaries and letters that will tell you what's in so-and-so's mind when he or she did something. I remember saying to my brilliant American history professor, Dr. Barbara Welter, "Was Edith Wharton an antifeminist?" Someone claimed this in a book review. Welter said, "What I know is she never signed an anti-feminist document." I think that's important. It had happened frequently in the early twentieth century, when women were trying to get the vote. But what interests me in history is the thinking: Why did someone do this or not? The why of events.

It's evident in the Madame Realism stories, because of the narrative structure, facts are absorbed easily. You've really experimented with this idea in most of your "nonfiction" projects. In "The Museum Hyphenated Americans," you were able to fit in this interesting fact within the structure of the piece that I really found fascinating. I didn't know the upper class bypassed the Island completely.

Yes. Exactly. I learned that while writing the piece.

I never thought about it.

I didn't as well. So, what interests me is learning facts about events that have larger implications.

I visited Ellis Island when I was ten. I also remember climbing to the top of the Statue of Liberty, which I don't think you can do anymore.

You can now, again. I never even wanted to.

Yeah. I don't know. I was ten.

No, no. People do that, but a lot of us New Yorkers don't. I've never been to the top of the Empire State building. I think people who live places often don't do what tourists do. To distinguish themselves from tourists. [*laughs*] I did go to the top of the World Trade Center, because one of the buildings had a penthouse restaurant.

Really?

Yes. Near the restaurant, there was an exhibition called *The Story of Gold*, the history of gold. I read that more gold had been mined in the twentieth century than in all the other centuries combined.

Wow.

Talk about raping the land, the resources, and value. That stayed with me. It's a fact, a fact with tremendous implications.

Also, where you encountered it . . .

Yes. *The Story of Gold* atop the World Trade Center. I don't know if I ever wrote about that.

IV. Afterlife

Academic Title ◯ **Editorial Direction** ◯ **Humor** ◯ **Voice as Force** ◯ **Predecessor** ◯ **Dialogue Style** ◯ **Desire** ◯ **The Interviewer** ◯ **Forming the Unknown** ◯ **Humility** ◯ **The Potential** ◯ **Breaking Paradigms** ◯ **The Anarchist** ◯ **Fear** ◯ **I Don't Want to Let Them Go** ◯ **Denis Johnson (Model)** ◯ **Relief** ◯ **Most of Us Disappear** ◯ **Relevance** ◯ **Mentors** ◯ **Immortality**

Taylor Lewandowski: *When did you start teaching?*

Lynne Tillman: The summer of 1993 at the Bard MFA. A couple of weeks before the session started, Leslie Scalapino, the poet, dropped out, because she had hurt her back, so I filled in for her. They asked me to stay for the last four weeks—another writing teacher had a breakdown. Bard was one-on-one meetings. At that time, the Bard MFA was something of a joke. There were only a few students I could work with. It was like a summer camp run by male counselors. About 1995 to 1996 it started to become a serious art school. By the time I left in 2003, it was a proper, lauded art school.

Yeah, I've seen some recent work at Bard. It looks great.

Oh, good . . .

So from there you went to Albany.

No. From there I was invited to teach one semester at Brown, and that's when I met Ben Marcus. I taught in the MFA program and one undergraduate workshop. I had never taught a workshop. I think that was the first time, or maybe the first time, was at Long Island University. It was miserable. There were too many people, and we only met for a week. After that I taught at Princeton for three years. I didn't like traveling there and back, but it was so well paid. Also, at this time our health insurance had gone up, and New York was becoming much more expensive. I taught there into the fall of 2001. I was on my way to Princeton on the day of 9/11. I stayed overnight at Paul Muldoon's. He was the chair then. The trains weren't running. I couldn't go home, and for a very brief moment, an instant, I understood what a refugee might experience. Very brief moment. Next morning it was running again. I knew I wasn't going to be rehired. Didn't have a big enough reputation, for one thing.

Around then Lydia Davis called me. We had met at Bard and become close. I revere her writing. And her way of being a writer, how she writes is one thing, but what she writes, what she lets herself do. Lydia once told me that if she has any interest in something, ridiculous as it might seem, she writes it down; she may write a story from it. I always stop myself. She has helped me, by saying, "Why don't you write that?"

Lydia had been asked to teach at UAlbany. She said she didn't want to teach full time, and I said, "Why don't we split it? I'll teach one semester and you teach another. If we can get health insurance, then I want to do it." So, she went to the department, and they agreed about this very unusual situation. On the day I was interviewed for the gig, I spoke with Bill Hedburg, who was in charge of systems—he may have run UAlbany, really smart guy—I said getting health insurance was necessary. Hedburg thought, and said, if he spread a one-semester salary throughout the year, he could give us health insurance. Then my sister Iris, who was editor-in-chief at UNC press, and aware of academic contracts, advised me to insist on an academic title, not just "writer-in-residence." She said, "Oh, no. You must get an academic title as well. Go in as an associate professor, and in three years you demand full professorship." So, I asked and they agreed.

Oh, that's smart. So, it's better to not be labeled as a writer-in-residence?

Right, because it has no academic standing. You might be treated differently. They agreed to everything. I started teaching in the spring of 2002. From Princeton to Albany in the same term, I was given a horrible schedule by a very mean professor. The woman didn't think the English department should hire living writers. She also didn't like it that I lived in New York City. To her, that showed I wasn't committed to the university. She gave me a schedule that included a Tuesday/Thursday class at 11 a.m. I had two courses to teach on Tuesday, nothing on Wednesday, and a class on Thursday, so I had to stay in Albany two nights, because the last train out of Albany was 7:15 p.m. My class wouldn't be over by then. It was so mean, but I won't mention her name.

Anyway, it doesn't matter. You wouldn't have heard of her. The new chair of the department was a terrific guy, but it was not a friendly place. There were people who hated each other, because they were in different disciplines in the English department. You know, the English wars. Faculty teaching literature versus writing versus theory, really crazy. Why not all, I thought naively. Then I realized it was institutional. They were fighting for their jobs. They needed students. Anyway, the chair said he'd change my schedule when he could. In my third year, I was teaching two workshops, three hours each, on back-to-back days, so I only had to spend one night. That was much better. Thank you, Gareth Griffiths.

Fundamental Reading

How did your approach to teaching change over those years?

I knew nothing about teaching a workshop. I had never taken a workshop. I never took any courses in writing.

Yes—that's strangely novel now.

There are too many MFAs now. You need to have a PhD to get a job, or at least it's better to have one, especially in English departments, because then you can teach other courses.

How did you approach teaching?

Badly at first. Group teaching is so different from one-on-one, obviously. There were many students in the English department when I began. The English department's enrollment has dropped by 30 percent. Maybe more, I'm not sure. We've lost many faculty positions.

It's a shame.

I used to have twenty-six people in a workshop. It was a nightmare. Sometimes it really matters who's in your class. My first workshop was made up of twenty-six business majors, who couldn't care less about writing. I had them read stories, write their own stuff, but a lot of that time is a blank—I must have repressed it. They were totally uninterested. I had a couple of students who showed talent. There was one kid who wrote like James Joyce. He became a scientist. He wasn't interested in writing. It was such a drag, having twenty-six kids in a workshop. I remember in a later workshop I divided them into five rows of fives plus one. They presented by row every week. I had them do a little conference where each row was responsible for a presentation. I told them I'm judging you on all of your work, so if someone doesn't pull their weight, it brings the rest down. I don't know why I didn't do that again. In my fifth year of teaching, the classes became smaller, which was such a benefit for me. I always gave them short stories to read at first. I always told them reading and writing must go along with each other.

You'd give them a diverse amount of short stories?

Yes, some contemporary, some not. Maybe Henry James, Edith Wharton, Kafka, James Baldwin, Flannery O'Connor. Hurston, George Saunders. *Pastoralia*—I loved that book. Amy Hempel, Lydia Davis, Denis Johnson, Deborah Eisenberg, A.M. Homes, Edward P. Jones, whose short stories are also wonderful. Others.

Do you think the workshop model is an effective way to learn how to write?

It can be. It depends on the students and of course the teacher. Lydia Davis and I both teach writing similarly. We're both sentence conscious. We're not teaching arc, plot development. If something like that isn't working or the characters do nothing, I'll comment on that, but it's how a story is written that makes the story. I was just reading a quote from William Carlos Williams: "It's not what we write, it's how we write it." It's of course a modernist point of view, but I think it's mostly true. You can write anything. You either write something in an interesting way or you don't.

Editorial Direction

You're both looking on a sentence-by-sentence level.

Yes and often word by word. My most well-known student is Nana

Kwame Adjei-Brenyah. His first novel just came out, but his first short story collection, *Friday Black*, came out a few years ago. Nana was in a mentor program in the English department as an undergraduate at UAlbany. I was chosen as his mentor. He reminded me of this in a piece he wrote. In our first meeting, and he was very shy, finally he hesitated and said, "I want to be a writer," and I asked, "What have you read?" That became our modus operandi. I'd give him stories and we'd discuss them. Then he took both of my writing workshops in his junior and senior years. He later thanked me for all the edits and comments on word choice, syntax, etc. He was avid and used my notes, queries, suggestions as heuristic devices. Some students are like that; they can be helped. You can feel that they are trying to absorb ideas about writing because in the discussions we'd be talking about issues not just germane to their stories. They listened, but you also have groups who don't—they learn nothing.

Humor

Teaching is a weird occupation.

Yes. Teaching is very, very strange. I've had wonderful moments. I had a student who came into my class wearing a hoodie, big guy, Black, expecting racism, which is everywhere, and walked immediately to the back of the class and pulled his hood over his face. He was going to sit there hiding, sulking. I said, "I can't see your face." I teased him a little bit about hiding. Soon he was sitting in the front of the class. Very near my desk. He became a beloved student. Really worked hard. He wrote me last year that he was now going to business school and asked if he could visit me. He did. It was wonderful.

I love that.

He had a stance: I'm going to fight you. I just wouldn't accept that. He was a lot bigger than me, but I wouldn't let him do that. [*laughs*] He allowed himself to be seen and heard. It was a great class in general. I tend to bring humor into my teaching. I am funny sometimes.

Often, I'd say.

Okay, often I'm funny. [*laughs*] I tell them on the first day: I don't care what you write. I care how you write it. You don't have to take this class seriously, but if you leave this university, and you don't know how to write a clear sentence, I pity you. I start out stern and gradually move to hilarity. Many of them later tell me it was the only class where they felt they knew the teacher and could speak honestly. The workshops have fewer students, and that's part of it. I usually feel at the end of the semester that most have learned how to write better. I can see it in their last stories. And, I've said this before, you don't teach talent. The people who have talent understand immediately why you've made a certain suggestion. They get it. They see it. But you can teach students to write better, to read with love.

Do you think teaching is an investment, a sort of extension of your legacy?

No to legacy, but in the one-on-one Bard MFA experience, I felt more immediately a relationship. That's one form of teaching, where you sometimes feel that what you're saying is helpful, and sometimes, as you know, they respond to a comment you said to them only much later. I think I've become a better teacher.

In workshop settings, working with undergraduates is more satisfying than working with graduates. They're less anxious. It's not going to be their career. They may not want to be professional or full-time writers, and they're taking it for many different reasons. That's more fun. Graduate students are very anxious. They're under a lot of pressure. They have an enormous amount to read. I can enjoy the group, but you can feel the pressure on them. With the undergraduates, I see in some of their stories that they paid attention and looked at my notes. I do line readings, and some of them absorb it; their writing does improve. I remember one student handed in his first story. Discussing it in class, I said something about, there's no sense of who this character is. He asked, "How do you write characters?" Which is, of course, one of the hardest things to teach. I said, "You learn how to write a character by reading." The third story he handed in was so much better. The class applauded him, and I asked, "What did you do differently?" He said he read. You can't write without reading. We don't pay enough attention to that relationship. Sometimes I know I've taught something. A student in class once remarked: "Obviously, hair flows from the head. You don't need to write that." [*laughs*]

All the writers I know read, love to read. It's part of writing. I tell students you wouldn't need me if you read a lot of good books very carefully. You learn how to write from reading, which is what I did.

I would also say, maybe not in the workshop, and I've been thinking about this lately, the idea of discussion or dialogue aids writing, or possibly the development in thinking and voice. I can see this directly in your practice. Conversation is another creative force.

Voice as Force

Conversation is meaningful to me, my work. I suppose you could link it to friendship. I have too many friends to mention, old and new friends, and they have all helped me learn and think. Their points of views are different. I also learn from conversations with strangers. I gave a talk at the Fales Library after they bought my archive, and some friends came to it. I spoke about how they had helped me become

a better writer. Their interests, what they thought, what work they made, helped me as a writer. Also, going back to the classroom, when the students discuss their work aloud, they learn by articulating what they mean. What works, what doesn't, and why. I don't just want to hear they like a story—tell us why. It helps students think about their own writing. Teaching is important, being taught. Some of my teachers and professors helped me way beyond their subjects. Dr. Barbara Welter, Mrs. Block, JJ Turner, Mr. Flanigan, Michael E. Brown, Miss Alexander. In all the schools I attended, there were teachers who helped me learn.

Some say you can't teach writing. You can't teach people how to make the rhythm of a sentence. You can't teach that. At least, I've never been able to, but I can show them when it's there and how to pay attention to it, and those who get it right away, as I said, usually have some talent, which is to say some capacity to understand what writing is and make their own writing better.

I could never be in a workshop. I would have been too insecure. Though I did take Harry Mathews's two-day workshop at the New School. He had developed a way to teach writing and passed it on to writer Lynn Crawford. That was fun. He gave us an in-class assignment, and I got so excited writing it, he had to tell me not to write so loudly. [*laughs*] Anyway, teaching can be gratifying, but often it's not and you cannot tell if you're helping people. Generally, I try to make them laugh.

I referenced this earlier in the context of your teaching, but what does it mean to leave a legacy?

Predecessor

I don't see myself as you see me. I don't think of my legacy. I have been told by younger writers that I've been important to them. You know what . . . I'm not even sure what legacy means. Let me look it up.

It's something transmitted from an ancestor or predecessor or from the past.

Well, I could say Jane Bowles's writing has affected the writer-me.

Her legacy has affected yours.

Dialogue Style

Okay—what she left. Legacy embedded in the work. Jane Bowles, I'll say again, gave me permission to deal with female characters in a very different way and still be considered or think of myself as a serious writer. There's so much prejudice. Too many writers who are women write conventionally about women, and it's uninteresting, at least to me, a certain complacency. Women have been assigned roles, and kept in place. Of course there's so much good writing, but Jane Bowles created something in modernism that veered away from it, and it is unique. She wasn't experimental in the same way as Djuna Barnes or Gertrude Stein. I'm sure she read everybody, but I'm talking about writers who were women who might have had an effect on her. The way she wrote female characters in *Two Serious Ladies* . . . Nobody wrote like that; her characters were out of this world. Also, her dialogue. I often don't like dialogue in novels and stories because it can be an easy way for writers to tell a story. She never did that. Her characters were as unique as their dialogue, dialogue was her writing. A friend of mine, I don't know how many years ago, said, "How do you write your dialogue? Nobody talks like that." I said, "I write the way I want people to talk." [*laughs*] In some ways I like D.H. Lawrence. I like his long passages of dialogue. In grad school, I read all of his novels and wrote a paper on them.

You wrote a graduate paper on him?

Yes. D.H. Lawrence because I took Sociology at CUNY graduate school, which meant I could do anything I wanted, and also read stuff I hadn't as an English major and American history minor, so it opened up a lot. Max Weber, for one. I was really interested in Lawrence. He started out with *Sons and Lovers*, which is autobiographical and very much about the working class. I thought his focus in the beginning was on class, but later on sexuality. He focused on relationships between men and women rather than on class relations.

I'd like to go back and read him again.

Well, his dialogue is intellectual, cerebral. They're talking about art, etc.

Yeah, I was really obsessed with him as a teenager.

I was reading him when I was young too. It made an impression on me. I think nineteenth-century writers had a better grasp on dialogue. They did it much better than many contemporary writers, because now dialogue is as ordinary as can be. Maybe because they talked more. It was their medium. Letters and conversation. When conversation is dull . . . I don't know . . . it's sometimes an effort to make conversation, but it's worth it. It is an engagement with other people. That's why I live in New York City.

I'm also thinking about Edith Wharton.

Oh, and she was born here. I love Edith Wharton. She has had a bad deal because of her class position. Her female characters are caught up in her period's social, cultural, and sexual mores. No one dismisses

Proust for that now. [*laughs*] The way she structures a novel, a story, brilliant. When she wrote about people who lived in poverty, they weren't types. The stories had compassion, an underlying sadness. There's a novella called *The Bunner Sisters*, which is marvelous. I remember the book had a pink cover. Anyway, back to legacy.

Desire

Well, it's interesting to talk about the difference between influence and legacy. So, I'm influenced by James Purdy or these writers I find guidance and direction, but legacy is something you are leaving behind for others intentionally or not. It's obviously in the physical books that you write, but also in teaching and moving through New York and the world in general with all your different friendships. It creates these spaces or opportunities to, yes, be exposed to another person's mind or creation, but also one that's transcending time and directing your life.

I think what younger writers, and artists in general, like about me, and maybe my greatest strength, is my curiosity—about ideas, people's lives, thoughts, people I'm talking to. I hope it's in the writing too. I'm genuinely, and I'm saying this maybe immodestly, eager to hear other people talk. I like to hear their stories, about their lives. I like the differences. People have lived such extraordinary lives. You can always find in a person's life many events or issues they have faced that are so different from your own, and that moves me a lot—hearing about someone who ran away from home, supported themselves, or someone who really loves their mother. I could go on with these differences.

People live in the most dire conditions and it's extraordinary when they can survive. Paula Fox, for instance, who I think is a great writer. I love her novels and there's one that I don't know if anyone reads, *The Servant's Tale*, which is so unusual. Paula came from the most rickety of family relations. She made the best of what she had. When she was little, she was taken care of by a neighboring farmer. He was really good to her and those years with him were incredibly helpful. Her life was very tough; her parents basically abandoned her, but she was more resilient because of him. Some people make a lot out of very little, and some people have a lot and can't make anything out of it.

That's definitely true.

The Interviewer

When someone interviews me, as you're doing, I'm interested in what's going on with you, like, why would you think that of me, or what are you doing in your writing and teaching and so on.

You're saying younger people are attracted to your sense of curiosity.

Yes. I think that's true.

I agree. You can't say every writer is like that or every artist is like that. It's certainly not true.

Far from true. [*laughs*]

Forming The Unknown

I do see it at times. I'm very much like that. Absorbent. I want to interact with the world. I recently had this conversation with a student, and I don't know if I told you this, but she's very introspective and always processing thoughts and emotions, very internal. She writes these intense stories and

essays with this advanced vocabulary. She's aiming for perfection, but it's an immature perfection, because her writing skills do not match the intensity of her thought life. One day during creative writing club, she asked me, "Why do we write characters that experience what we have not?" It's a fascinating question.

It is.

The beginning of my response was: "How often do you walk through the hallways and think about what other people are thinking? How often do you wish you knew what was going on inside another person?" She replied, "All the time." In my mind, for me, this is a person that's a born artist.

It's almost embarrassing to talk about yourself. I may have said this to you. I also think the fact that I've been in some form of psychotherapy, that I've usually had a person with whom to be as honest as I can be and discuss some awful issues and ugly feelings, has helped me not talk about myself as much. I have less need to.

Humility

Being in psychoanalysis enabled you to move beyond yourself.

I have an outlet. It may be true, although I know people in analysis as long as I've been in analysis who talk about themselves incessantly. But maybe in my case there's my family structure where I was the youngest by a number of years, listening rather than talking, and also felt what I said wasn't important. I was listening to protect myself.

That makes sense. When you first talked about this, I was surprised when you mentioned early on in your writing you felt very insecure and lost until you found a different literary community inside the art world.

Well, there was that, but that wasn't what really helped me. It was therapy. I was as threatened or frightened by artists as I was by other writers and particularly writers who seemed to have a lot of self-confidence. But I was . . . I couldn't write, I think, because of a particular feeling I inherited from my family, a threat to my existence if I became a writer.

Well, writing and psychoanalysis allowed you to live, right?

Absolutely.

Without those, it is difficult.

When I was living in Europe, I would start a story and never finish it, or anything, except when I was asked to write about porn films or something that didn't matter to me. I wanted to write fiction and I had no support. I knew if I never went back to New York, I would never become what I wanted to be. A writer. When I returned, that was my goal. I knew I needed therapy. I certainly knew I needed to be around people who were talking in a way that was familiar to me. I needed to be around the rhythms of American English. I came back to New York at a very good time. As I said, there was a lot happening. Maybe every young person who comes to a city like New York or LA or wherever they feel comfortable gets that sense, but in New York what was happening interested me; I was already excited by art and film. I had already developed some strong interests. Looking at a photograph, film, a painting—and installations were new to me. It was all encouraging and funneled directly into my writing.

The Potential

Yes, that idea of looking at a photograph, a painting, a sculpture, that encouraged you. It's related to all these different facets. I want to go back to that idea you and I disagreed on. Do you remember our conversation about the potential? I talked about it as someone moving toward this idea of a true self, and you described it as a widening of opportunities.

Before we get to that, I want to say the word "courage" is in the word "encourage." I think about that a lot. For me to develop courage, I needed to be encouraged. So to support your argument, I could say I always wanted to be a writer, right? I moved as much as I could. I moved as many obstacles as I could, which I mean my neuroses, and moved enough of them, and I still have quite a number but not so stultifying, so I was able to get to the point where I showed people my writing. I would often be in terror, shaking like a leaf, but I did it. Then I started to publish and started to publish more. There's a way in which you have a grandiosity that mixes with paranoia. First of all, you think people are going to hate this—that's grandiose. It's paranoid that you think people are thinking about you. Really no one cares. You're not going to get attention. You're not going to have people throwing stones at you. These are internal feelings that don't really have to do with reality, or the reality of the world you live in. People might think your writing is shit—usually they don't come up and tell you.

I had an experience years ago at the very first reading I gave, which was from *Weird Fucks*. It was at the Ear Inn. Poet Ted Greenwald was curating that event. I was drinking scotch for weeks beforehand. Taking valium. [*laughs*] Just to calm down. It turned out many friends from Europe were in the city at that time. It was a full house. I forget who I read with, but it was really good. It was encouraging, but *Weird Fucks* was seen as really strange by a lot of people. No one was writing that way. It wasn't considered avant-garde because it was narrative.

Later, in a Madame Realism story, my retort to that rejection of narrative was: "a story is a way to think." Probably no one noticed. [*laughs*]

I was sure *Weird Fucks* was good writing. That's the funny thing. Even though I was very insecure, I was also secure. I don't think I could have gone on if I didn't think the work was strong. I told you what a poet wrote me, right?

No, I don't think so.

Well, she had a small press then and I sent her the manuscript of *Weird Fucks,* and she wrote a letter, for which she apologized years later, saying "cut it with anything, pages from the telephone book." To fragment it, that's what so-called avant-garde people were doing, so she saw *Weird Fucks* as conventional. You live in conditions, a time, with certain paradigms until those paradigms are broken.

That's it. You live different paradigms until they are broken.

Yes. Reading Thomas Kuhn's theory on paradigms and shifts, that was helpful.

I think that's what I'm thinking about. Some people can escape that, but others cannot.

Breaking Paradigms

That's right. I don't know where it comes from. There are many writers who have gone against those paradigms. I felt strongly, right or wrong, about my capacity to think differently, or I needed to think differently in order to write what I wanted to write. I remember writing *Haunted Houses*, and I might have said this to you. I finished the first three chapters, which went into section one, and knew you were supposed to bring the characters together, but I couldn't think of a reason why. There was no reason why I should bring them together. Truly, that's what I thought. It would be artificial, arbitrary. "Should they meet in college or a bar? Why did they have to meet?" I asked myself a question and couldn't answer it. It didn't make sense to me, so that made *Haunted Houses* difficult to sell until someone saw the value in it. In my very next book, I did something totally different from *Haunted Houses*, which was to work with coincidence so that many of the characters kept bumping into each other. I used this for a special effect about the experience of my characters, drifting. Coincidence is not supposed to work in fiction, but one thing about traveling around is that you meet other travelers more than once. There's always a circuit, or when I was traveling around Europe. I saw writing as the only freedom I had.

You gained the confidence.

The Anarchist

Well, it wasn't even confidence at that point. It was almost like the anarchist in me.

The anarchist?

Yeah. The anarchist. I was rebellious. I did things against fear. I wasn't going to let it stop me though I was often obstructed neurotically. But I wasn't going to become a conventional "woman." I wasn't going to be a man or a woman, neither was what I wanted to be. I didn't like the attributes. I didn't want to be masculine or feminine. I wanted to make my own decisions, even if I didn't know they were decisions. People do this with their lives, make decisions that don't seem important at the time. That's why I'm interested in other people's lives. Decisions have unknowable consequences, and the younger you are the less you are aware of consequences. It really hits you hard when you realize the effect of past behavior. It's a terrible awakening. There's not a clear line between insecurity and confidence. For instance, recently I was asked to do a walk-through for Ed Clark's show at Hauser & Wirth. I was honored to be asked, but I had never done a walk-through, and I was really scared. I have a certain understanding of paintings. I'm not an expert. I'm not an art historian, but I've certainly thought about painting a lot. I was terrified, but what did I do? I studied.

What was your process?

I read the catalog that Hauser & Wirth put out, which was incredibly helpful. I went to the gallery where the show was on a few times, and looked at the paintings and took notes. I gathered my thoughts over a month. It was like a cram course on Ed Clark, but I was very nervous about it. I didn't want to do it, because I was afraid. Because I was afraid, I knew I had to do it.

That's a big shift.

Fear

Fear is a real destroyer. People talk about the fear of failure or fear of success. It's a little too general, because fears develop in relation to and from very specific points in their lives. So these blanket interpretations—someone could say I'm afraid of succeeding. Well, what the hell does that mean?

That is very general.

Or, I'm afraid of failing. Well, just think about Beckett. Fail again. That's always there when you're writing anything. You sense it could fail. No matter how many books you've written. It's always the next project. If you become complacent, forget about it. Absolutely, forget about it. You can sometimes feel a writer's anxiety in the work.

What do you mean? Can you think of someone specific?

Oh, obviously Kafka.

[laughs] Definitely.

He's the granddaddy. His work is about anxiety, always doubting what he was doing. I wish more writers had those doubts. I just finished reading *The Copenhagen Trilogy*. It's a very anxious book. I think it's brilliant. There was only one moment when I thought it could've been better. I read Blake Butler's book *Molly*, and we did a conversation at POWERHOUSE Arena. It's an upsetting work. As writing, I don't know if it's his best writing because the reality about trauma is its repetition, and so it's kind of constraining. Blake had to repeat the same questions and worries about Molly, he wants to supply her needs and help her. He tries to help her, and then the horror and shock about Molly's suicide. That upends him completely. How did he live through this? How did he go on? Again, curiosity about someone's life who's experienced something terrible is fascinating. Maybe ghoulish. But the response to his complex work has been, from many women, and some men, who knew her or her poetry—she was a well-regarded poet—very disappointing. He shouldn't have written about her, and not about how she treated him, her betrayal of him also with other lovers. No, he shouldn't have dared. Of course, women writers have no trouble writing about their difficult partners, cheating husbands, famous or not. The reverse sexual prejudice is . . . thoughtless. Literally, without thought. Molly's suicide devastated him. Why can't he write about that?

I agree. It's very difficult in a way, but also we need the flexibility of language to express the difficult or perhaps otherwise unsaid. I personally have been thinking about death a lot lately. I found out Tuesday morning one of my past students passed away.

No.

Yes, so this week has been tough.

Of what?

He fell asleep and didn't wake up.

Oh my god. How horrible.

It's mysterious. He had a lot of gender issues, depressive. We'd have conversations about music. I once saw him at a local punk show, but very disconnected at school. I could tell he struggled on many levels. It's fucked up. I think I've cried every day this week.

So sad.

Sixteen.

Terrible. The thing about getting older that you never think about is how many people you know who die before you.

It's scary.

I Don't Want to Let Go

David Rattray, Paula Fox, Susan Hiller, Craig Owens, my friend Joe Wood. He was quite young. He fell off a mountain. It's still horrific to think about. Joe's a character in a novel I'm writing. On and on. Harry Mathews. Callie Angell, John Michell. Heathcote Williams. Many more. People with whom I had conversations and relationships. It's shocking the number of people you love who eventually disappear. It accrues, one death after another. The part of your life associated with them vanishes, not exactly in memory or how they affected you. I want to keep these people in my mind. I don't want to let them go. I don't want to forget them. I want to keep them in the present. I miss those conversations. And as usual when someone is no longer around, you think, "Why didn't I ask her this?" or "What did Harry really think about that?" You know what you know, and what you don't know or what you didn't ask, it's too late. Or what you didn't say becomes more profound. In a way, there's a sort of numbness that comes over you: yet another death, yet another death.

How did you meet Paula Fox?

At a reading we did together. *No Lease on Life* had just come out. I had heard of Paula, rather recently, but never had read anything. She read from her third novel, *The Widow's Children*. Jonathan Franzen, who'd helped revive her career, introduced her. Her reading just totally knocked me out. Afterward I went up to her and said how great it was, and she said something nice about my reading. Then I decided to read every novel she'd ever written, and did. I phoned Betsy Sussler, *BOMB*'s editor-in-chief, and said I want to have a conversation with Paula Fox. Don't let anyone else do it, please. I was adamant. Betsy was great about this kind of thing—suggestions based on your enthusiasm. I recommended other writers to her also.

When Colm Tóibín's first novel, *The South*, came out in the US in 1990, I asked to interview him for *BOMB*. It was his first US interview. Name spelled wrong. [*laughs*] He and I met in 1990 because we were published by Serpent's Tail at the same time, and we did a tour together. I won't go into that, and besides Colm wrote about it. That English tour was crazy, no one liked what I read, but we became close friends. Something good came out of it. I don't want to be in this world without his voice in my ear.

I was fortunate to do an in-depth conversation with Paula about her novels. We became friends after this. I visited her in Brooklyn often and came to know her husband, Martin Greenberg, a philosopher and translator. We'd go out for lunch. We always laughed a lot.

Paula had had a tough life, and never complained, never seemed bitter about her books not getting the attention they should have. Her writing was not about her; it was about what she may have experienced, but always in relation to other people, transformed by her great interest in other lives and cultures. I invited her to visit a class on the short story I taught one semester at Columbia. She read to the students and talked to them so generously. Even though her eyesight was rapidly decreasing from macular degeneration, and was using a big magnifier to read, she agreed to do a reading with me at McNally Jackson. I forget the year. There wasn't enough light, older people need much more light to read by, so I stood beside her holding a strong flashlight that Wally Shawn lent me. He and Debbie Eisenberg were in the audience, and that was a thrill. I was holding the light, when suddenly Paula turned her head and kissed me on the cheek. I cherish that. So surprising, and rare. Thinking of her and that moment makes me happy and sad. Her eyesight and memory failed more and more. The last time I went to visit her, she'd forgotten I was coming, and she was humiliated. I told her it didn't matter, we all forget. But I didn't try to visit her again. I think she was not able to be herself. Paula was always herself. I didn't want to upset her.

And Denis.

I knew Denis Johnson only five or six years. I wish I could have known him forever. He was an exceptional human being and of course a wonderful writer. He led a very different life from many other writers. He stayed away from the parties. He didn't live that kind of writer's life. He didn't want it. I guess he didn't need it, and he needed to protect himself, because he once had such a drug and alcohol problem. Also he was very sensitive. I met him in Japan. We were invited to Kyoto by the journalist, Riyo Niimoto, who had once lived in New York City. He had interviewed Denis and me, among many others, and he liked us, and he made a book of interviews about American writers' political thinking. He invited us to Kyoto where he was going to start an MFA program. It'd be the first in Japan. He wanted us to talk about MFA programs and writing, read from our work, and that's how I met Denis. Our first meeting was not exactly great. I arrived in Tokyo, got on a train to Kyoto, or maybe a train then a bus, I forget. Everybody told me how difficult it would be to get around because of the language barrier, but everyone helped me. It was absolutely fine. So, I got there . . .

What year is this?

Denis Johnson (Model)

2011. Not long after Fukushima, far from Kyoto. Denis passed away five years later. So, I arrived and they are all at a café bar waiting for me. I sat down with the host and Denis and Cindy Lou, his wife. I had taught some of Denis's stories, of course, in my undergraduate writing workshop. He said something about he how didn't know my writing; he had looked at a picture of me and thought I'd be too intellectual;

he wouldn't understand me. I was pissed off. He realized when he said this, it was insulting. The next morning at the hotel he made every effort to be warm and friendly. When he realized I didn't have this huge ego, that I lived in the universe he lived in, he changed his behavior. So we became friends. I wish we would've known each other much longer.

He taught me something that was very human. Several of the Japanese writers we met were young women and they all seemed to have written twenty books. [*laughs*] One night we were all, American and Japanese writers, going to a gathering, a party. One of the women writers was very beautiful. And she didn't come to it. Denis was disappointed, and said she hadn't come because she was interested in him. Or attracted. I said, but she's married and has a child at home. Denis looked at me and said, "Don't rain on my parade." That taught me something. We have our fantasies. It's fun to imagine they're true, like I could've been a great tennis player. [*laughs*]

Denis told me a lot about himself. He was very warm. It's interesting that he was short, and, you know, I'm short, and he wasn't as short as I am, but I remember walking beside him and not having to look up. [*laughs*]

That's a change!

It was really something in his favor. A lot of people I knew and loved towered over me, especially Craig Owens. When Denis came to New York, we always met up. He said to me one time, "You really are a good friend." I was so happy. I learned later he read very few contemporary writers, almost none. It was another way to protect himself. I did tell him he had to read Mavis Gallant. Absolutely. He told me he did and liked her work. Of course, he would. Great writer. Then I understood why he didn't read my work. He did hear me read from *American Genius, A Comedy*. We continued to correspond until a month before he died. A year before he said his cancer had returned, but he never said that it was bad, he was dying. He didn't tell anyone except his wife and family. Very private. His students adored him. At the memorial at 92nd Street Y, a number of his students spoke. They loved him.

He's a real model, in my mind of a writer, or at least a writer in sobriety.

He was a great writer. In many ways, I wish I had much less need for the life I have. I go see plays, shows, galleries, in conversation with loads of people. For me, it's generative, I'm not a chitchat kind of person. I can do that if I have to, but it bores the hell out of me. I want to talk about something. So, anyway back to the dead . . .

You talk about people you don't want to forget, but in Mothercare: On Obligation, Love, Death, and Ambivalence, *observing and reflecting on the death of your mother. It's different.*

Yes. Her illness first. I didn't have any experience watching someone die. I could have been there for David Rattray, who as you know, was extremely important to me. I don't know what happened to me, Taylor. Sometimes your own behavior is so strange. As I said, Susan Hiller first encouraged me as a writer when I was living in London. Then, it was David Rattray, even though I hadn't written anything to show him until *Weird Fucks*; that's when I spent a lot of time with David and years later, I met Eileen Myles, but in terms of his death . . .

I fell away. He had separated from his wife, who was a really nasty person, then after years he went back to her, so I was pissed off. I didn't see him for a few years, which I regret. She was just horrible, and horrible also after he died. Semiotext(e) was bringing out the first

Madame Realism book, edited by Chris Kraus, and she asked me, "Could we do a joint book party with David Rattray?" She was also publishing Rattray's *How I Became One of the Invisible*. I reluctantly said yes. But because of this, we became friends again. I was very happy about it, though it was never the same. And my fault. Maybe we didn't have enough time, maybe we would have if he had enough time.

On Christmas Eve, he phoned me, which was very surprising. He wanted to tell me that he was in the hospital and had a brain tumor. He was so generous. He didn't want me to find out from anyone else. I was shocked. I told him I'll visit tomorrow. So the next day, Christmas, I did. His head was wrapped up because of the operation to remove as much of the tumor as they could, but he told me he wasn't going to survive. I couldn't believe it. His brother also died of cancer. I was stunned. When he came back from the hospital, I was afraid to get in touch with him. I really behaved so strangely, and to this day, I don't understand why. He was living with his wife, but that wasn't the reason.

One day not long after, I was on the street, and you know he lived around the corner from me (Avenue A and 11th Street). I saw him in a car—his head was bandaged. I tried to hide, and they found me. David had to talk to me, he wanted to. I went over to their apartment and we spent an hour together. He was still very much David. He wasn't wasted away or anything. We talked about his poetry. He showed me he was revising some poems. We had a lovely time. It was us again. But I was afraid. I couldn't handle the fact that he was dying. Then I never saw him again because he moved out to the Hamptons where his family had a house, or his sister did. He's from an old style, upper class American family. He was the wild one. Stayed in the Beat Hotel in Paris in the 1950s. A bad boy. Meanwhile translating Artaud. He was a polymath, one of the most erudite people I knew. He was an essential part of my intellectual life. I think those people are a loss of a different sort: Susan Hiller, Craig Owens, Joe Wood Jr., David . . .

Relief

In comparison to Mothercare, *witnessing your mother's illness and death seems like a very different process.*

That's right. It's different when you take care of someone for a very long time. There's emotional relief, then a great deal of grief. I didn't have that. I had the relief, but not the grief. The book is very different from my other books, but then most of my novels are different from each other.

It's a full-length nonfiction essay. It stands out. It's different.

I didn't want to call it a memoir, because I don't think it is. It's a very specific moment about a relationship, an event not about myself but my mother's illness. It's very different. If it were a memoir, I wouldn't have written about taking my mother to the toilet. I wrote it because I had learned things about the health system, what the pitfalls were. And also to forget; writing helps you, anyway me, to forget. What do you think of the differences between my novels?

We've talked about this a little bit. We did find a through line. You're exploring different ideas for each novel, but there is this wrestling with perception, or a preoccupation with consciousness on the page. Why is it truly impossible to know another? This seems to be in a lot of your work. This impossibility to see the world through another person's perspective. Where does this anxiety originate from? It permeates through your work. You see it in Cast in Doubt, Men and Apparitions.

Also, *American Genius, A Comedy.* When we find out her name is Helen. It's not that you can't present a different point of view, but there's a difference between representing another and knowing a character or person in the same way you know yourself. What is their motivation? Why did they do this? Another person's reasons, certainly their unconscious, are not available to you. Unless a close friend calls up, tells you their dream, and how they're associating to it, then you may find out more about their interior life. People bore you or always surprise you. [*laughs*] A best friend can turn. The problems I've had with my family, with one sister especially, have been damaging. Hurtful. When you think you know somebody, and you discover you don't, or when you realize they don't know you, have no idea who you are, it shakes up, even shatters, your sense of perception, and how you understand the world.

Has that happened to you a lot?

Some. I think I'm a trusting person. I like people. I love many people. I trust you. Why should I trust you? You could have conversations with other artists or writers, and they might be much more cautious than I am. I don't expect you to write about me in a way that is nasty or to reveal things that I don't want you to reveal. Why do I trust you? I tend to trust, but given my family, shouldn't. [*laughs*] David, my insignificant other, is much more cautious than I am. That's always been the case. Often people open up to me. I'm not disloyal. If someone says this is a secret, not only do I suppress it, I don't remember it! [*laughs*] There was a lot of anger and distrust in my family, and I discovered later many issues, especially about the lie of loyalty. Loyalty almost became pathological. There was something wrong that I don't want to talk about. I have felt betrayed by a few friends. Friendship is complicated. You don't sign a contract. It's supposedly voluntary. Stuff happens that you don't expect. You don't know the unspoken, you can only imagine. Friends' feelings can be hidden. Mine also. A lot has to do with trust. Trust is necessary, and not easy to establish.

Most of Us Disappear

On this idea of perception, or historicizing consciousness on the page, fictional or not, I wonder, what do you personally wish to leave behind?

I hope to be remembered as someone who helped others. Obviously, I'll leave behind some books. They may sit in a storage unit, or they may stay out in the world, but usually writers disappear. Their books disappear until someone revisits them. Most authors' work doesn't stay around. I remember learning that lesson when I was reading *Americans Abroad* in Amsterdam. There were so many American names I didn't recognize, except a few because the Europeans were still reading them, like Horace McCoy, who was a mystery writer, or Harry and Caresse Crosby. It was a very in-my-face lesson that most of us disappear. The idea one has a legacy and will be remembered— if you're writing to be remembered, forget about it. I don't think you choose to be a writer, or at least I didn't choose to be a writer. I felt I had to be. I originally thought I wouldn't care how others respond-ed to my writing or if my books were not in bookstores, because I read literary histories. I thought I was prepared to be an unknown. [*laughs*] But to write no matter what.

You were preparing to be unknown?

Yes. I thought I was. When I was a junior in high school, I wrote a paper on reputation. I researched Chaucer and learned that he was a mentor to a poet, John Lydgate. After Chaucer died, Lydgate dropped the way Chaucer's work should be recited. He dropped the final "e." So the rhythms were wrong: "Whan that Aprille and its shoures soute." That last e should be pronounced "ah." Chaucer's work was forgotten, and Lydgate was *it* for two hundred years, then Chaucer came back, and who's Lydgate? There I was, sixteen and thinking about reputation.

I've said this before. When your first book comes out, and you think it's going to make you so happy—yes I've finally been published—but in fact that's when the melodrama begins because you do want people to read it. You do want to get reviewed. You do feel competitive and all sorts of other lousy feelings you don't want to feel. And when you were writing, you were much happier. People who are not writers or artists think the world you exist in is glamorous or seriously wonderful or whatever. In a way, it's like any other job, but it can be more public—your successes and failures. What is success? In a way, you could say I'm successful just because I am published. Definitely fortunate. But there is a lot of disappointment being a writer or an artist. You decide, you do it, no one asked you. There is a lot of rejection.

I remember years ago my agent Joy Harris gave a party for the inimitable literary critic Michael Silverblatt to introduce him to editors so they'd send him touring authors for his wonderful radio program, *Bookworm*. I was the only writer invited because I had met Michael in LA. I walked into the room, and everyone there was an editor who had rejected one of my books. There was one who hadn't, so I walked over to him, told him that, and talked with him. [*laughs*] You're a writer. You're on your own. Some have money, connections, but that kind of support doesn't keep you writing. It's a need.

So, what is success to you then?

For a long time, I didn't even think I wrote the books I wrote. I'd look at them on the shelf or I'd hide them away so I didn't have to see them anymore. Did I really write this? I couldn't write the same book again, so it seemed impossible to me. I don't think I'm alone in this. It's taken me a long time to know that I've written my books. The fear I have is just the futility in writing. You need to do it. In my case, I have to do it, otherwise I'd be bored to death. I'm working on something now and feel it can be nothing, or mean nothing, to anyone else. So, what's the point?

That's a dangerous question, but still an important question.

Relevance

Yes, but the feeling, as I was saying, is of shock once the book is published. You don't expect, or at least I didn't expect to have such strong emotions. Some of my writer friends are more indifferent or secure about their work, or less concerned, say, about reviews. I have felt closer to this as years go by and more time in psychoanalysis. I know writers who don't read their reviews. That's fantastic. Good or bad. They don't look at them. I wish I had that kind of strength. Caryl Phillips, whose writing I love, doesn't read them. I bet Denis Johnson didn't. I don't think he saw himself in a community of writers. He saw himself as alone. I feel much more involved with other writers.

Well, that's a big difference and also has its own advantage, which I'm sure is also connected to a writer's longevity: how much they give back or provide space for others. Personally, I consider your work and your personality, what you have accomplished, as exciting, fresh, in contrast to other writer's attitudes or postures.

That's good to hear! I hate it, but I like flattery. [*laughs*] I wanted to say something more about disappointment and its opposite. Because I have been helped in what's called a career by more people than I can name, but most importantly my agent Joy Harris. I've been with her since 1988. When my books sell poorly, and most have, other writers have told me to switch agents, but I never have. Because I know what my writing is, I know it's not Joy's fault. My writing isn't going to be popular, not going to sell a lot. She's good, I love her. I used to read chapters of *Haunted Houses* to my great friend Patrick McGrath, who brought the Gothic back. Ann Patty at Poseidon published *Haunted Houses* after nineteen rejections. Early on, Ira Silverberg was a supporter. He and Amy Scholder ran Serpent's Tail in New York, and reprinted *Haunted Houses*. Richard Nash lifted me up when he published *American Genius, A Comedy*. This was 2006. No one other than Richard would touch it. It was sent to four editors, one of whom wrote back, an important woman editor, "I don't know what Lynne is trying to teach me." I mean, really, would she write that to a male writer? Prejudice kills me. Richard kept me going, brought out books no other press would do. Andy Hunter, when he was at Catapult, helped my book *Men and Apparitions* come into the world. And now Mensah Demary at Soft Skull. And I have to mention Peninsula Press in the UK and Will Rees. A book of mine hadn't been published in Europe for twenty years. And boom, I'm up from the dead. So over time, people have supported and helped me. Still, being an accomplished artist is not a permanent position. [*laughs*]

Like Denis Johnson, you are a model to some degree for me and other writers. Do you know Juliet Escoria?

I know who she is.

I talked to her once and she was reminiscing on early aughts New York City when she attended a lot of readings and wrote about them for Electric Literature. *She always praised you as the best writer she encountered.*

I didn't know that. I was so surprised by the publishing world and those it elevated. I thought of myself entering that world from the back door. I didn't have people in my family who could have helped me. I didn't know anyone at *The New Yorker* or *The New York Times*. But I wanted to say something about my father, who didn't have that clout, but without his being in my life . . . it's hard to say it. I don't think I would have become a writer. Maybe survived. I felt his love, neurotic as he was. I felt his interest in my mind. He loved to play. We watched sports together. He read to me at night. When I was in college, he wrote me letters. In one he said, "You have a special intelligence." I didn't know he thought that.

Mentors

Wow.

Returning to a writer's life without an MFA. I didn't have professional mentors. People, like me, had to figure out ways to meet writers. Meeting David Rattray was terrific. Whether he was published or not, he was a great writer, intellectual, and a lot of fun. He never complained, Taylor. I wish I could be more like that. He never talked about being recognized or whatever. He could've been a son of a beloved mother who loved him madly and given him a lot of confidence. I don't know. He found a kind of balance and more contentment with time. He never laid his problems on you. Conversation made him happy—in that way I think I'm like him. I hope so.

In the mid-1980s, I went to hear Etel Adnan read at the CUNY Graduate Center. Ammiel Alcalay phoned and said you must go, so I went. Her reading just astonished me. Her language, the lyricism, the insights, philosophical prose and poetry, so I was bold and went up to her afterward. Somehow she agreed to meet with me when she came to New York the next time. And that started our conversation. And Etel wrote wonderful letters. Simone Fattal, a sculptor, an artist and her longtime lover/partner, had a press that published everything Etel wrote. She'd send me Etel's books and I'd send her mine in return. Etel was known only as a poet then—I didn't know she was also a visual artist. She was relatively unknown. When Negar Azimi asked me to write something for *Bidoun*, a magazine focusing on Middle Eastern artists, I suggested a conversation with Etel and spent two days with her in Sausalito. Even Negar didn't know who she was. *Bidoun* published it, then somewhat later *Bidoun* put her in a show in London. And boom.

In her mid-eighties, she was heading to fame and many shows. Etel told me, the last time I saw her, that it had become too much for her. Everyone asked for work, and she couldn't produce like that. Etel was an exceptional person and artist. Knowing her was, and not to be corny, though sometimes I can't help it, knowing her was a gift. Talking with her. Her compassion, her intelligence, her worldliness.

Conversation is important. I know writers need support, especially starting out. I like to be helpful. I'm fighting against feeling that I have no value, that I'm not worthwhile. That's a common trait. I try to be worthwhile to others. I try to help others. I'd also like to be remembered as a person who has a smart sense of humor. Often ironic, though it's regularly not in favor. Irony is political, used in the best ways.

Etel and David and Susan and Paula and Joe and more—I learned from them.

Immortality

Justin Taylor has been that for me. In some ways, we survive or continue or live from the past to the present and on. I think about the writers you've mentioned. Their lives and literature intersect with your own and create a different, alternative route, which provides real purpose—this expansion.

It's interesting you say that. When *What Would Lynne Tillman Do?* came out, I did a reading at McNally Jackson. Essayist Claudia Roth Pierpont was there and bought a book, and said something like, the writers and artists you write about are off the beaten path. I hadn't thought about it that way, because they were my beaten path. [*laughs*] There are way too many to add, but it includes: James Baldwin, Woolf, Barbara Pym, Jean Rhys, Freud, Colette, Stein, Joseph Roth, Mishima, Mann, Flaubert, Kafka. Kafka! Students ask me, who have you read, which is the question I asked Nana. And many theorists, other than Freud. He's the best writer of them, except for Foucault, Jacqueline Rose, Erving Goffman and Clifford Geertz, Woolf, and Walter Benjamin, Barthes. And what's great about books, about reading, is you keep finding writers you love. It keeps you alive. Agota Kristof, too many to name, and of course, living writers—I could cite many more—and there's always Kafka . . .

Can't forget about Kafka.

Who can?

No one.

Also, discovering Mavis Gallant.

All this consciousness widens how we interact with the world.

Yes, I hope so.

That's the purpose of literature.

Yes, maybe. If it needs a purpose. [*laughs*] But yes to knowing and feeling outside yourself, and for another's pain. And pleasure . . .

I Wish I Had More Time:
On Lynne Tillman and Psychoanalysis

Claire Donato

When I scheduled a time to speak on the phone with Lynne Tillman about her engagement with psychoanalysis, I suggested that we speak for an analytic hour—forty-five minutes. "I might need an analytic forty-five minutes," she joked. The irony of my recording our interview using computer software called QuickTime was not lost on me, nor is this quote from Tillman, in conversation with Lewandowski: "I'm interested in so many different things. I wish I had more time."

After we spoke, I wished we had more time, more analytic hours. Tillman is generously candid, unpretentious, funny, and easy to talk to. Her multidimensional oeuvre draws from her speaking voice, a peculiar mix of Long Island-cum-NYC dialect and cosmopolitan wit. It's a refined and articulate way of speaking, which has served her as a writer and interviewer who's engaged countless painters, writers, and other artists; and as a near-lifelong analysand—where that voice, under the treatment of numerous clinicians across a span of decades, was set free.

When Tillman was growing up as a child in Woodmere, Long Island in the 1950s, two of her relatives—one a teenager—were in psychoanalysis four times a week. At that time, it was unusual for middle-class families to have children in psychoanalysis, but Tillman's parents "were not opposed to anyone going into psychotherapy or just therapy. They didn't think it was shameful to speak about," she says. Still, this decade wasn't an ideal time for young women to be in psychoanalysis. With the misogyny of the day making its way into consulting rooms, young women were often particularly unsafe in treatments with their male analysts.

Tillman recalls a vivid memory—she was ten years old and "wrote in [her] little diary that [she] was depressed." In Lewandowski's conversation with her, she also shares that she wanted to be a writer from the age of eight. So she had the terminology down, and was already reckoning with having a melancholy consciousness through her words from a young age.

In her first semester of college, Tillman was in treatment with a male psychologist (not a psychoanalyst) whom she says "was not great at all." His name was Mr. Williams—he did not have a doctorate—and, to quote Tillman, he "had no idea what a young girl with my ambitions and depression and issues around sexuality [was going through]." Alienated by work with him, Tillman wound up talking to him mostly about American history, which was her minor in college.

Subsequently, during a difficult time as an undergraduate, when she was between institutions (she transferred from Hunter to SUNY Binghamton back to Hunter College) and especially depressed and overeating, she began seeing an older woman who "basically kept [her] alive." She wasn't an analyst, but she was wise and alert—Tillman began to trust her and slowly found her footing as a young adult.

After graduation, Tillman moved to Europe for seven years, where she continued to repeat patterns that had been haunting her. "I wasn't getting away from what I needed to get away from psychologically, which was my family," she explains. She also wanted to write fiction but, as she says to Lewandowski, she had trouble finishing stories and "had no support" there. When she came back to the States, she knew she needed therapy and began to see a psychoanalyst-in-formation, a former book editor who was enrolled as a candidate at a training institute. In our conversation, Tillman uncharacteristically referred to this clinician by her first name despite the fact that she calls all of her other treatment providers by formal monikers: Mr., Mrs., Dr. "I never call my doctors by their first names, because they are different from me. And I want that distance. They're not my friends," she says. Was this clinician an exception to this rule because she was once part of the literary world?

It was under her care that Tillman began writing *Haunted Houses*, whose title refers to H.D.'s *Tribute to Freud*, in which H.D. writes: "We are all haunted houses." Tillman occasionally read chapters-in-progress from *Haunted Houses* aloud in the consulting room. "I was unable to show my work to anyone," she says. "I think reading it to [my analyst] was really helpful to me."

One day, the therapist had a stroke in the consulting room, for which Tillman was present. "I was lying on the couch, and I knew because she slurred her words," Tillman says. Tillman told Heather she was having a stroke, and the two argued about it. Because Heather did not go to the hospital right away, the stroke caused significant damage to her brain, which led to an eventual termination of Tillman's psychoanalytic treatment with her. "It was very, very disturbing," Tillman says. "And so for a while, for a few years after that, I didn't see anyone."

The events narrated in *Mothercare*—Tillman's painstaking daily care for her aging mother, with whom she had a fraught relationship, and who was diagnosed with normal pressure hydrocephalus, a condition that took her through the perils of America's medical industrial complex—eventually led Tillman back into psychoanalytic psychotherapy with Dr. Stanley Grand. (She dedicated her essay collection, *What Would Lynne Tillman Do?*, to him and so has agreed to my mentioning his name.) Dr. Grand was a past president of the Institute for Psychoanalytic Training and Research (IPTAR) and chair of its ethics committee, a faculty member in the NYU postdoctoral program in psychotherapy and psychoanalysis, and a member of the Contemporary Freudian Society. Tillman worked with Dr. Grand until he passed away in 2018. In his Legacy.com obituary comments, one former patient writes that "his gentle care and treatment saved [his] life."

"There's much I did not write about in [*Mothercare*]," Tillman says. "It was abysmal, but that's not the story I wanted to tell. I wanted to tell the story of what happens when suddenly a parent, a lover, a friend gets sick—you don't know what it is; you don't know how to deal with anything. It's just all thrust on you." To Lewandowski, she adds that she wrote this book to forget—"writing helps you, anyway me, to forget."

Beyond *Haunted Houses*, Tillman's engagement with the psychoanalytic field runs through all of her prose. Freud is frequently quoted by Tillman's critical alter ego, Madame Realism, and is read and studied by the central ethnographer of *Men and Apparitions*, Zeke (who himself is an analysand). And if "we are all haunted houses," as H.D. posited in *Tribute to Freud*—if "a person [is] a ghosted house," as Tillman posits in an interview with *The Brooklyn Rail*—then it seems apt that *American Genius: A Comedy* ends in a seance, wherein a group of artists (or possibly mental patients) begin to unearth their deepest traumas.

Tillman's psychoanalytic novels—*American Genius, A Comedy* and *Men and Apparitions* in particular—distinguish themselves from psychological novels because her psychoanalytic novels deploy rigorous free association. In a 1991 interview on *Bookworm*, Michael Silverblatt refers to Tillman's work as following chains of consciousness, as opposed to streams, "by which I mean that the associative process [seems] very intense, very directed, sharply edited," he says, also noting that her books seem to operate "by a string of memory, and in this way, [. . .] [seem] to have an ulterior inner method."

In a movement in *American Genius, A Comedy*, a wound is invoked that transmutes from something "more internal" to a scratch on the narrator's leg at summer camp in the past, to a different scratch on the same leg from a cat in the present that becomes "an unsightly scar. It [hides] something terrible, though wounds are not supposed to be obscene." The progression of this image feels emblematic of the way language continuously unfolds from itself in Tillman's psychoanalytic novels—and in conversation with her—like sentence origami or a multi-layered quilt.

New York City is in the midst of a psychoanalytic renaissance, with new training institutes burgeoning and a plethora of Lacanian artists prowling about to become "psychoanalysts-in-formation." In my mind, no artist feels as attached to the lived experience of being in psychoanalysis as Lynne Tillman, who writes novels that critics have long-remarked are characterized by free association, dexterous wordplay, and interior monologue. Indeed, just about everything Tillman writes feels like it comes from the mind of an analysand. As *Bookforum* critic Michael Wood has remarked, Tillman's characters are "made up of words." But what does this actually mean?

As Tillman writes in "Madame Realism in Freud's Dreamland," originally published in *Art in America*, "Freud wanted to dig up the past, to unbury torments, exhibit them and make them disappear or lose their power." Her body of work does something similar. In "The Unconscious Is Also Ridiculous," a character fantasizes about the life she could have had as a famous tennis player, and mourns the fact that "if her parents had recognized her gift and gotten her a great coach, she could have won the Open, and maybe a Grand Slam." And in her novella *Weird Fucks*, Tillman's narrator unflinchingly shares details regarding her sexuality and experiences with sexual boundary violations: "I awoke in the car which was parked next to a field," she writes. "After he raped me, he said, 'Now we go to my sister's house.' [. . .] He thought, because I hadn't resisted, that I liked it." By conjuring these demons, Tillman expels them, finds an antidote to them and, as she says in *The Mystery of Perception*, "[lets] 'em loose."

In *The Mystery of Perception*, Tillman reflects on how losses accrue over time, as well her desire to hold the dead in mind, to not let them go. She remarks: "The thing about getting older that you never think about is how many people you know who die before you. [. . .] There's a sort of numbness that comes over you: yet another death, yet another death." Tillman's terminated clinical treatments mirror and complicate the losses she narrates in conversation with Lewandowski.. They strike me as microcosmic rehearsals for life's many endings. And it's Tillman's metabolization of these losses—her ability to mourn— that makes her wise, and reflects her engagement with psychoanalysis. Because, as she notes in a conversation with with *Granta* editor Josie Mitchell, "In a sense we are always haunted by our past and what psychoanalysis is, for me, is not about cure but about understanding those ghosts."

You Could Do More With This

Emily LaBarge

For some years, I have kept a LYNNE TILLMAN folder. Added to on a semi-regular basis, it includes things such as:

People are desiring machines, sure; we're also meaning machines. We put things together, even though we're often wrong.

I regularly question my preferences. Why I like or dislike writing, a photograph. I don't trust experience, even if it has shaped me; I don't fervently trust what I think or believe, while I believe it still.

What separates me from the world? Secret thoughts? [. . .] Out of nothing comes language and out of language comes nothing and everything. I know there will be stories. Certainly, there will always be stories.

Books are not mirrors, and life doesn't go onto the page like life, but like writing.

With bigger brains, people have concocted notions about self-reflection and self-awareness, which allowed for "I think, therefore, I am." Not "I think what; therefore, I am what?" One would have thought that might matter.

I don't want to take a position. Not taking a position is a position that acknowledges the inability to know with absolute surety, that says: Writing is like life, there are many ways of doing it, survival depends on flexibility. Anything can be on the page. What isn't there now?

Everything is a problem in some way, I can't think of anything that's not a problem.

The folder is highlighted green, which means *ACTIVE*, as in regularly added to, interacted with, underway, ongoing, and additions come from sources across her oeuvre of seven novels, five short story collections, four works of nonfiction, and dozens (could it be hundreds?) of essays. Like the long, generous, deeply intimate and funny interview with Taylor Lewandowski that you have just read, my LYNNE TILLMAN folder is as capacious and curious and sage and varied as Lynne Tillman, the living person, not the folder, although I suppose in a way she lives somewhere between who she is and what she has written. Her words issue forth into the world and touch minds near and far, become talismanic, guide writers who hope to be as prolific and enduringly interested in the mystery of life as she. The life of the mind has an afterlife, an afterglow, sometimes even an aftershock, and no afterword could ever hold all that.

I first met Lynne on the page, in the searching, perspicacious mind of Madame Realism, who wandered the halls of art galleries and museums, the streets and bars of New York City, or sometimes just stayed at home in her apartment, reeling from a dream in which she seemed to have turned into a Jeff Koons sculpture—all bulges and grotesqueries, mismatched parts, shifts in scale and perspective—or some other misadventure. Madame Realism, no matter the circumstances, was wry and funny, knowing and astute, and committed to looking long and hard, thinking longer and harder. Taking everything seriously while really not taking anything too seriously, because the project of life, or whatever we want to call it (living?), is long and there is much to see and even more that will remain unseen, just out of grasp (but we can try).

In her conversation with Taylor, Lynne quotes Kafka's statement about education: "My education has damaged me in ways I do not even know." She continues, describing her experience of living in Europe as an American, and how quickly she realized her world had been formed in a very particular way and required reforming, decentring. She explains, "It's about de-education, or recognizing your thoughts are not your thoughts." I would describe this as in many ways the project of Lynne's work: to remake the minds of her readers, to show them that they don't know what they don't know, that there are infinite ways of being. These infinities are proposed, in fact, by writing—form, structure, language. As Lynne says in one of her essays about Andy Warhol, writing is different from life itself, even when it traffics in representation, which Lynne's work never does in conventional ways.

What happens, happens in language: "It's how a story is written that makes the story," she tells Taylor, describing how she and Lydia Davis share an approach to their métier as writers who teach. "We're both sentence conscious. We're not teaching arc, plot development. If something like that isn't working or the characters do nothing, I'll comment on that, but it's how a story is written that makes the story." Or as she talks about recently rereading a quote from William Carlos Williams (you will find in interviews and conversations that Lynne is always rereading, close as ever, not afraid to revisit and find something new or changed in an old source, friend, memory), "It's not what we write, it's how we write it."

Lynne's work is objectively different at many turns, but it is always the same in that it is marked by an interest in consciousness, by which I mean what it is to be a person—a problem with no answer, but which bears repeating and asking as much as possible. In this beautiful meeting of minds, Taylor and Lynne, you can find much information about wild and wonderful things: John Cale, Lou Reed's "Sunday Morning"; gay clubs with chicly suited men dancing; Simone de Beauvoir witnessing a Tillman family row in a Paris café; the first art and experimental cinema in Amsterdam (run by Lynne and a friend); David Rattray; Kathy Acker; London and Europe in the 1980s; New York at any time; what it's like to live with a Bass player; what it really means to have a restless, ongoing, infinite fascination with the world and a talent to portray it that remains entirely unique. But you can also find, again and again, a mind at work, an investment in instability and not-knowing, a belief that every new thing can be different. "I always wanted to change it up and give myself another problem," she says, just like her protagonist, Helen, of *American Genius: A Comedy*.

The second time I met Lynne was in person, almost a decade ago, when she acted as an examiner for my PhD, half of which focused on the "earth-body works" of Ana Mendieta, whom Lynne had known adjacently before the young artist's untimely death in 1985. "I was at the trial," she told me in the first of many moments in which the breadth of her lived experience of culture contributed to my understanding of a person, place, or thing as alive long after it no longer is. "You started out as alongside art," Lynne says, of her desire to connect with people, to converse. "We are alongside it, sometimes in front of it. We aren't making the art. You're not in it, you're around it." In her writing, you also *are* it, *become* it, and it becomes you, just like Madame Realism taught me that she (and I, you, we) could ourselves be a form of exegesis.

During my exam, when the inevitable question of readership arose, Lynne told a story about the filmmaker Trinh T. Minh Ha, who, when asked a hostile question by a man in the audience after a screening, said: "Who are your films *for*?" "She said," Lynne recalled, "I make films for sensitive people." Lynne looked at me in a knowing way, like I understood this too, like maybe we were sensitive people together, "and I just thought that was great." She smiled. At the end of the day,

Lynne handed me her reading copy of my thesis. It had been torn from its vinyl cover into chunks that looked a convenient size, perhaps for subway reading, or any other kind of transport. They were put back in the wrong order, frayed, covered with handwritten notes, and sprouted pieces of green paper with additional notes where the margins had proven insufficient. I still have them all, in my LYNNE TILLMAN folder, and at least one of them changed my life. A simple statement, almost a throwaway, was written and then underlined on one of the flying green sheets: "*** you could do more with this." A great mantra for any writer, and a hallmark insight from a great writer who has never stopped doing "more with this" at every turn.

"You can't write without reading. Somehow we don't pay attention to that relationship," Lynne tells Taylor in their sweeping conversation, filled with a lifetime of precious insights. "All the writers I know love to read. It's part of writing. I always tell them you wouldn't need me if you read a lot," she continues. When she says "them," she means the students she has taught at SUNY Albany and the School of Visual Arts, New York, but many of us who have never been in her classrooms might consider ourselves tutees, too. "You learn from reading, which is what I did," she says. True, but we learned from reading Lynne, reading her a lot, reading her to learn how to write and to think and to live—and we do need her, need to keep reading her, always will.

Notes

from "The Funniest Person I Know"

1. Lynne Tillman, *No Lease on Life* (Harcourt Brace, 1998), 79.

2. Sigmund Freud, *The Joke and Its Relation to the Unconscious*, trans. Joyce Crick (Penguin Books, 2003), 84.

3. Lynne Tillman's column "In these Intemperate Times" was published in *Frieze* from 2011 to 2018.

4. Lynne Tillman, *Weird Fucks* (New Herring Press, 2014), 33.

5. Tillman, *Weird Fucks*, 51.

6. Reiner Stach, *Kafka: The Decisive Years*, trans. Shelley Frisch (Princeton University Press, 2013), 163-64.

7. Stach, *Kafka*, 258.

8. Brod, Max. *Franz Kafka: A Biography.* Schocken Books, 1960, 178.

9. Steve Lipman, *Laughter in Hell: The Use of Humor in the Holocaust* (Jason Aronson, 1993).

10. Lynne Tillman, "What I Know For Sure About Laughing at Myself," *Oprah.com*, June 15, 2011, https://www.oprah.com/spirit/laughing-at-myself-lynne-tillman-someday-this-will-be-funny

11. Tillman, "What I Know For Sure About Laughing at Myself."

12. Lynne Tillman, *Motion Sickness* (Red Lemonade, 2014), 113.

from The Mystery of Perception

1. Lynne Tillman, "Nothing Is Lost or Found: Desperately Seeking Paul and Jane Bowles," in *What Would Lynne Tillman Do?* (Red Lemonade, 2014), 37-48.

2. Lynne Tillman, "Lynne Tillman on How Feminism Has Affected Men," interview by Holly Connolly, *AnOther Mag*, November 13, 2020, https://www.anothermag.com/design-living/12950/lynne-tillman-on-how-fem-inism-has-affected-men-men-apparitions-interview-2020.

3. Ariana Reines, "Interview with Ariana Reines," interview by Rebecca Tamás, *The White Review*, July 2019, https://www.thewhitereview.org/feature/interview-ariana-reines/.

4. Lynne Tillman, "Writing 'Alongside'—Not 'About'—Art: A Conversa-tion with Lynne Tillman," interview by Craig Owens, *Los Angeles Review of Books*, May 1, 2019, https://lareviewofbooks.org/article/writing-along-side-not-about-art-a-conversation-with-lynne-tillman/.

5. Craig Owens, *Portrait of a Young Critic* (Badlands Unlimited, 2018).

List of Images

1. Eileen Myles sitting on Lynne Tillman. Unknown. Fall 1982. The Fales Library & Special Collections, MSS. 180, Box 13, Folder 34. (p. 15)

2. Paranoid's Ball. The Fales Library & Special Collections, MSS. 180, Box 33, Folder 34. (pg. 24)

3. David Rattray Postcard from Hawaii. Unknown. 1977—1985. The Fales Library & Special Collections, MSS. 180, Box 13, Folder 34. (p. 27)

4. Charles Henri Ford & Lynne. Unknown. The Fales Library & Special Collections, MSS. 180, Box 9, Folder 10. (p. 31)

5. Lynne Tillman Age 8. Nathan Tillman. 1955. (p. 33)

6. Kathy Acker & Lynne Tillman in Frankfurt. Dirk Görtler. 1993. (p. 40)

7. William Kennedy. Lynne Tillman. 2022. (p. 45)

8. Lynne Tillman & David Hofstra. Chie Narita. April 11, 2019. (p. 48)

9. David Hofstra. Unknown. Late 1980s. (p. 52)

10. Americans Abroad Manuscript. Franklin Furnace Exhibit of Rare Books. 1973. The Fales Library & Special Collections. MSS. 180, Box 26, Folder 3. (p. 54)

11. Buffie Johnson, Lynne Tillman, Paul Bowles in Tangiers, Morocco. 1987. The Fales Library & Special Collections, MSS. 180, Box 9, Folder 6. (p. 57)

12. Library of Congress Copyright Letter for *The Collected Works of Jane Bowles and Two Serious Ladies*. 1986. The Fales Library & Special Collections, MSS. 180, Box 26, Folder 46. (p. 59)

13. Lynne playing football. Nathan Tillman. mid-1950s. (p. 62)

14. John Cale & Lynne Tillman. The Fales Library & Special Collections. (p. 76)

15. Andy Warhol. Stephen Shore. 1996. The Velvet Years Promotional

Acknowledgements

This book has shaped my life in unimaginable ways. Every trip to New York City to speak with Lynne or rifle through her archives at Fales Library reoriented my life. It sounds hyperbolic, but it isn't. I remember first talking with Stephanie LaCava at the Odeon the day of our reading in 2022. (Thank you, Stephanie!) I had first envisioned this as an interview for *The Paris Review*, but they were not interested, so I reframed my original idea through the framework of Sylvère Lotringer's early Semiotext(e) books, especially *David Wojnarowicz: A Definitive History of Five or Six Years on the Lower East Side* and *The Accident of Art*. I'm forever indebted to Sylvère. I did not start reading Hans Ulrich Obrist's interviews until the book was finished, but his own insistence on longform interviews as a specific genre, which usually spanned years, sometimes decades is another simpatico approach.

This book would not exist without the careful, considerate, and generous attention of Nicodemus Nicoludis, whose early enthusiasm over Lynne's *Madame Realism* sparked an interest in this project and a quick bond between us. As well as Naomi Falk and Chris Molnar at Archway Editions, who have encouraged, designed, and even housed me over these last couple years. Thank you!

I also would like to thank Andrew Durbin, Claire Donato, and Emily LaBarge for their wonderful essays; K.O. Nnamdie, whose conversations and exhibitions have been transformative, not only in terms of this book, but profoundly in my life; Brady Laughlin, who is really a grounding force for me in Indianapolis and knows me better than anyone; Henry Crawford and Phoebe Temkin for their friendship and occasional inspired texting; Rick Petaccio for always providing a place to stay and comedic, fever-like monologues; Nik Slackman for the encouragement and photo scanning; Susanna Cuyler for everything; Anika Jade Levy for also letting me stay amidst a busy week; and Justin Taylor, whose friendship and writing keeps me sane.

But this entire project would not exist without Lynne Tillman. I am beyond grateful for her generosity to work on this collaborative interview over the last three years. I had no idea meeting her at KGB would result in this singular object of shared consciousness. I do hope this book serves as a distillation of her life, thought, and a companion to her astonishing oeuvre.

MORE FROM ARCHWAY EDITIONS

Archway Editions is a literary imprint of indie art book publishing company **powerHouse Books**, and is distributed to the trade by Simon & Schuster; our books can be found in fine indie bookshops around the world, or Amazon if you must.

To learn more about **Archway Editions**, please visit here:

...and stop by our sister imprints **powerHouse Books**:

...and **POW! Kids Books**:

For trade queries, visit Simon & Schuster:

Send us love letters, mash notes, or mindless musings to:
- comments@archwayeditions.us
- or by tethered phone line @ 212-604-9074 x 104
- or by postal delivery to our publishing HQ in Dumbo, Brooklyn:
  Archway Editions
  c/o POWERHOUSE Arena
  32 Adams Street
  Brooklyn, NY 11201

Or alternatively to our research lab in Industry City, Sunset Park:
  Archway Editions
  c/o POWERHOUSE @ IC
  238 36th Street (bldg. 2)
  Brooklyn, NY 11232

LYNNE TILLMAN is a novelist, short story writer, and cultural critic. Her novels are *Haunted Houses*; *Motion Sickness*; *Cast in Doubt*; *No Lease on Life*, a finalist for the National Book Critics Circle Award in Fiction; *American Genius, A Comedy*, and *Men and Apparitions*, nominated for a Republic of Consciousness Prize (UK, 2021). Her nonfiction books include *The Velvet Years: Warhol's Factory 1965–67*, with photographs by Stephen Shore; *What Would Lynne Tillman Do?*, a finalist for the National Book Critics Circle Award in Criticism, and The Broad Picture. Her essays and stories are published in various journals including *Frieze*, *Bomb*, *The Whitney Review*, *Bookforum*, *Aperture*, *Artforum*, *N+1*, and in artist's monographs and gallery books such as those of Dana Schutz, Steve Locke, Stanley Whitney, Amy Sillman, and Raymond Pettibon, and in museum catalogues inculding The Whitney Museum of American Art; The ICP Boston, Hammer Museum, and MOCA. Tillman has received a Guggenheim Fellowship; a Creative Capital/Andy Warhol Foundation Arts Writers Grant, and was awarded the Katherine Anne Porter Prize by the American Academy of Arts and Letters. Her most recent work is *Mothercare*, an autobiographical book- length essay. In 2025, Soft Skull Press will publish her collected stories, *Thrilled to Death*. In 2026, Zwirner Press will publish a collection of her essays on art and culture. She lives in Manhattan with bass player David Hofstra.

TAYLOR LEWANDOWSKI has work in *Bookforum*, *Interview*, *The Whitney Review of New Writing*, *November Magazine*, *Los Angeles Review of Books*, and others. He has curated two exhibitions, *Leaving*, which explored the complications of returning home, and *Pathology*, a collection of his grandfather's crime scene and autopsy photos from the eighties, which culminated in the book, *Pathology* (Nighted, 2020). He created SMUT, a queer dance night in 2022, which featured DJs, like Him Hun and ASL Princess. His story, "This is How You Burn Away," was recently included in the first Car Crash Collective anthology. He teaches at Herron High School in Indianapolis and co-owns Dream Palace Books & Coffee.